CONNIE ARMSTRONG HOLDS HER DAUGHTER, CHELSEY, AT KINGS LANDING HISTORICAL SETTLEMENT.

TRAVELING

Keeping pace with the Kicking Horse River, vehicles sweep westward through Kicking Horse Pass on the Trans-Canada Highway. Each year some 1.25 million persons travel this section of the highway, which traverses the mountain wonderland of British Columbia's Yoho National Park.

By William Howarth
Photographed by George F. Mobley

Prepared by the Special Publications Division

THE TRANS-CANADA

From Newfoundland to British Columbia

National Geographic Society, Washington, D.C.

TRAVELING THE TRANS-CANADA
From Newfoundland to British Columbia

By WILLIAM HOWARTH
Photographed by GEORGE F. MOBLEY

Published by THE NATIONAL GEOGRAPHIC SOCIETY
GILBERT M. GROSVENOR, *President and
    Chairman of the Board*
MELVIN M. PAYNE, THOMAS W. MCKNEW,
    Chairmen Emeritus
OWEN R. ANDERSON, *Executive Vice President*
ROBERT L. BREEDEN, *Senior Vice President,
    Publications and Educational Media*

Prepared by THE SPECIAL PUBLICATIONS DIVISION
DONALD J. CRUMP, *Director*
PHILIP B. SILCOTT, *Associate Director*
BONNIE S. LAWRENCE, *Assistant Director*

Staff for this Book
PAUL MARTIN, *Managing Editor*
JOHN G. AGNONE, *Illustrations Editor*
CINDA ROSE, *Art Director*
STEPHEN J. HUBBARD, *Senior Researcher*
DIANA VANEK, *Researcher*
PATRICIA N. HOLLAND, M. LINDA LEE, *Research Assistants*
LESLIE B. ALLEN, RICHARD M. CRUM, CATHERINE HEALY,
    M. LINDA LEE, JANE R. MCCAULEY, TOM MELHAM,
    THOMAS O'NEILL, *Picture Legend Writers*
JOHN D. GARST, JR., ISAAC ORTIZ, ROBERT W. NORTHROP,
    JOSEPH F. OCHLAK, DANIEL J. ORTIZ, MARTIN S. WALZ,
    Map Research & Production
ROSAMUND GARNER, *Editorial Assistant*
SHARON KOCSIS BERRY, *Illustrations Assistant*
JANE H. BUXTON, H. ROBERT MORRISON,
    Editorial Consultants
JODY BOLT, *Consulting Art Director*

Engraving, Printing, and Product Manufacture
ROBERT W. MESSER, *Manager*
GEORGE V. WHITE, *Senior Assistant Manager*
VINCENT P. RYAN, *Assistant Manager*
DAVID V. SHOWERS, *Production Manager*
GEORGE J. ZELLER, JR., *Production Project Manager*
GREGORY STORER, *Senior Assistant Production Manager*
LEWIS R. BASSFORD, *Assistant Production Manager*
MARK R. DUNLEVY, *Film Archivist*
TIMOTHY H. EWING, *Production Assistant*
CAROL R. CURTIS, *Senior Production Staff Assistant*
SUSAN A. BENDER, LESLIE CAROL, BETSY ELLISON,
    KAYLENE KAHLER, SANDRA F. LOTTERMAN,
    ELIZA C. MORTON, *Staff Assistants*
ANNE K. MCCAIN, *Indexer*

EAGER HOUNDS OF THE LANGLEY, BRITISH COLUMBIA, FOX HUNT CLUB FOLLOW HUNTSMAN JERRY REEMST.

COAST TO COAST

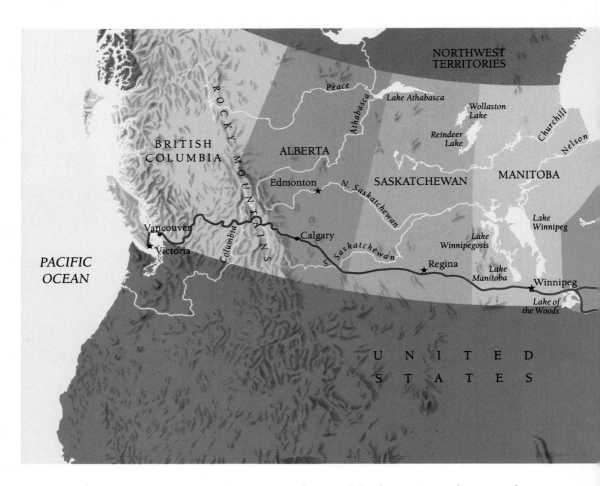

Thin strand that knits a nation, the 4,800-mile
Trans-Canada Highway crosses the ten provinces
on its way from St. John's, Newfoundland, to
Victoria, British Columbia. Officially opened in 1962,
the highway affords travelers an intimate view of a
sprawling land—a country peopled with a rich
diversity of cultures and blessed with some of North
America's most spectacular scenery.

Canada's Maple Leaf flutters above an independent
confederation of provinces. Though its titular head
remains the Queen of England, Canada charts its
own course as a parliamentary democracy.

ON CANADA'S MAIN STREET

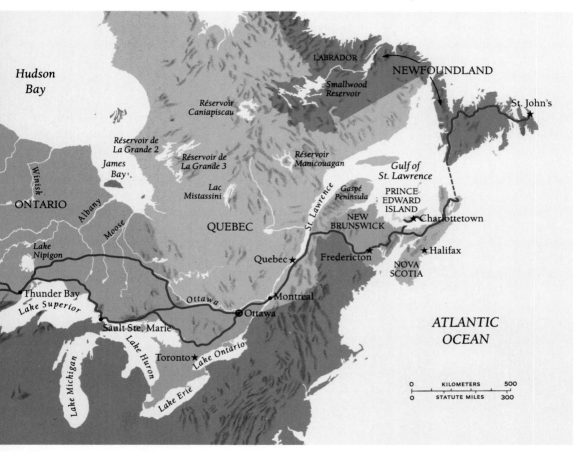

PROLOGUE

WHEN I WAS GROWING UP in Illinois, summer meant a time when my family piled camping gear in the car and drove north. We started before dawn, my parents sharing the wheel while kids drowsed in the back among fishing poles. Miles went by, as fields gave way to upland pastures, then to lakes and dark evergreen forest. We entered Ontario and still drove north, through deep wilderness to a major east-west highway. Young hitchhikers often stood at that corner with signs: "Going Trans-Canada." Our car went north, but I always wanted to turn.

Now at last I have taken that journey down the world's longest national road, the Trans-Canada Highway. Winding across all ten Canadian provinces, the Trans-Canada carried me from the Atlantic harbor of St. John's, Newfoundland, to the Pacific shore at Vancouver Island, British Columbia. For its entire 4,800

miles, the highway offers an all-weather surface with wide shoulders and mostly gentle grades. That achievement is an engineering marvel, since the Trans-Canada crosses some of North America's most challenging terrain.

Along my route I saw the road leap Atlantic inlets and flank the broad St. Lawrence River, then span a thousand miles of glacier-scoured rock and muskeg to reach the rolling central plains. From grasslands I climbed the Great Divide and crossed its icy mountain roof, then descended through desert canyons and rain forests to the Pacific. With side trips, I traveled more than 20,000 miles, most of it in a small camper van, my rolling home with stove, bed, and well-stocked icebox. At times I had the company of my family or photographer George Mobley.

On this transcontinental crossing we saw every extreme of geography—and frequent

Part of the rich Canadian mosaic, costumed staff members chat at Old Fort William (opposite), a reconstructed 19th-century fur-trading center at Thunder Bay, Ontario. Fans spread in graceful gestures, Korean dancers (below) perform at Vancouver's Asia-Pacific Festival, which celebrates the roots of a large number of Canadian immigrants.

changes in climate. "The True North," as Canadians call their country, has no shortage of frost and wind, but also plenty of sunshine. On summer days I drove through wilting heat and humidity, then slept under cold, starlit skies. Canadians use a Celsius thermometer, for which I devised a shorthand scale: 20 warm, 10 cool, 0 misery. The natives are thick-blooded optimists, accustomed to inclemency. As snow pelted my windshield one morning in June, the radio announcer chuckled: "Well, that's Canada; there's no written guarantee on the weather here."

Even more varied were the people I met, bits of the human mosaic that forms Canadian culture. The national languages are English and French, making Canada one of the world's few officially bilingual nations, but I also met native speakers of Gaelic, Hindi, Ukrainian, Low German, Finnish, Japanese, and Athabascan.

Canada contains more than 90 cultural groups; today one of every six citizens was born abroad. To this nation of immigrants the Trans-Canada is a Main Street, linking some 30 urban centers.

The highway passes along Canada's developed southern corridor, where three-fourths of the country's 25 million people live. But even that land often seemed big and empty. Many days I drove across immense forests and plains, with only power poles for companions. Along the Trans-Canada I followed the route of history, from the earliest landfall by Vikings in Newfoundland to the sprawling fur trade empire built along inland waterways by French and English forces. Rivals for centuries, those two factions have long resisted the growth of a single national culture.

Canada is no melting pot, people told me, yet time and again I saw signs that a broad new

identity is emerging. The Trans-Canada has played a primary role in this change, for its opening in 1962 bound the nation together. Railways launched continental trade, but the road has united a people. Once isolated villages now have highway access; students drive to distant provinces to attend universities. Commerce flows east and west today, as people change jobs and traverse regional boundaries.

To be sure, many of the old provincial ways endure; often I felt I was crossing ten separate countries, each with its stubborn customs. The Newfoundlander has never lost his Irish brogue, while villages in Quebec raise tall cathedral spires, for 90 percent of the province is Roman Catholic. Ontario is English Canada, with white-steepled chapels for Anglicans and Presbyterians; in the prairies, Hutterites and Mennonites pursue their plain, time-honored ways. Out

west, the traditions come as roundups and rodeos, threshing bees or the annual salmon harvest.

A resistance to change explains Canada's style of governing, which retains in Parliament the trappings of a colonial past. Still, a new constitution emerged in 1982, now finally ratified by all provinces, and today Canada clearly possesses a strong national government. Its armies have fought bravely abroad and maintain a firm defense; the Royal Canadian Mounted Police are respected enforcers of law and order. In Saskatchewan I visited their training division, where one recruit studied my camera and made careful notes. "I've been instructed this week," he said, "to observe seven suspicious incidents."

I felt that sort of wariness often, whenever Canadians talked about the United States. We share the world's longest undefended border and the largest bilateral trade, with Canada now

Young cowpoke holds tight aboard a high-kicking steer (opposite) at the Calgary Exhibition and Stampede, Canada's biggest rodeo. Below, a Newfoundland fisherman works a cod trap in the bountiful waters off Petty Harbour, near the eastern end of the Trans-Canada Highway.

earning substantial profits from its U.S. investments. Yet time after time I heard complaints that Canada was a laggard compared with its hustling neighbor. "You get things done," an Ontario businesswoman told me. "We just sit around the campfire and talk." That old image of being slow to change endures, like all traditions, even as evidence piles up that Canada is a nation bursting with vitality.

Canada's trains and planes run on time; cities gleam with new buildings and well-kept parks. And yes, the streets are clean. On a per capita basis, Canadians live longer and experience less divorce or violent crime than their U.S. neighbors. Canadian teachers are well paid; conversation flourishes; radio plays great music and serious dramas. This high standard of living, not measured strictly in earnings or tax credits, affects the pace of life—steady and understated,

like the modest "Limited" in every corporation's name. Given these virtues, and Canada's superb outdoors, it's no wonder tourism is booming.

On my journey I found that Canada is more than the symbols it preserves, such as the scarlet-coated guards at Ottawa. To me, this country once seemed so near and familiar, the source of cold fronts and Christmas trees, of summers passed at a lakeside cabin. But the highway took me across a land where discovery never ends. Canada is both very old and ever new, the birthplace of North America's past—and the continent's youngest nation. In Newfoundland, I met a trucker who drives the Trans-Canada regularly, coast to coast in five days. "I'd like to take it slower," he told me. "There's a good deal of country out there I've never really seen." I took to the road with that goal in mind—to slow down and explore this big, open land.

MEDFORD TAYLOR

Strolling back in time, a villager passes St. Mark's Chapel at Kings Landing Historical Settlement, a re-created home of Revolutionary War-era British Loyalists from the United States. Costumed families and some 50 buildings give visitors to this New Brunswick town a glimpse of rural life in the 1800s. History entwines the four provinces of Atlantic Canada, pervaded by the tang of a maritime tradition.

ALONG

BOB SACHA

EASTERN SHORES

Atlantic Provinces

O n my first evening in Newfoundland, I drove straight to the top of Signal Hill. Sunset had begun to tint the town of St. John's, as shadows slipped down bronze streets and pastel-painted houses to reach a blue harbor. The west darkened, but in the east a strange brightness spread above the sea. A dense fog bank had formed, lifting a white curtain that reflected the sun back to shore. For a long interval the day would not die, and that became my image of the enduring Atlantic Provinces.

I had come to Newfoundland to begin my Trans-Canada journey in leaps and bounds, for the highway cannot link these four widely separated provinces. Jumping from here to the Maritimes—Nova Scotia, Prince Edward Island, and New Brunswick—the road hurdles a broad stretch of northern ocean. The sea joins the Atlantic Provinces; it has shaped their shorelines and moist, cool climate, marked their passing days with currents and tides. This world endures, perhaps, thanks to the salt in its veins.

On my flight to St. John's, I discovered that the natives don't say NewFOUNDland but Newf'nLAAND, a drawn-out sound that slightly juts the jaw. To most Canadians this name refers both to Newfoundland and Labrador, which entered the Confederation together in 1949. Natives here regard Labrador as a chunk of mainland wilderness; Newfoundland is their island home anchored far offshore, only 1,900 miles from Europe.

On Signal Hill I was closer to Dublin than Denver—and a half-hour off from everywhere. Newfoundland lies so far east that it has a unique time zone, 30 minutes ahead of Atlantic Standard. The North American day dawns here, and so did New World history. Around A.D. 1000 a party of Viking explorers came ashore on the northern peninsula and camped at a grassy cove, L'Anse aux Meadows. John Cabot hove up to the eastern shore in 1497, and English boats routinely fished the Grand Banks before Shakespeare was born. In 1583 England claimed Newfoundland as its first overseas colony, an act that launched the British Empire.

Since then many seekers have passed through this portal, from immigrants bound west to pilots braving the first Atlantic flights. When I left Signal Hill that night the lights in St. John's were gleaming. All around me lay a black void of sky and ocean, save for one flashing airliner far above. It passed out of sight beyond Cabot Tower, which bears a plaque commemorating this northern gateway: "Near this spot Guglielmo Marconi received the first wireless transatlantic message on December 12, 1901."

Next morning I ran some errands and began to see the "foreign" side of Canada. The prices were all in Canadian dollars and cents, but each required translation: At a 35 percent premium, minus discount and commission, how much is that in *money?* Every item wore three different labels: English, French, and metric. Hence grapefruit was pamplemousse, and six made up a kilo. Local shoppers tend to ignore the French, since 98 percent of Newfoundland is English-speaking.

A special breed of English I soon discovered, in such new expressions as "wicket" (bank teller's window), "gandy" (pancake), and "hydro" (electricity). Newfoundland has a dialect unto itself, spoken with a musical Irish lilt and a large measure of "Newfie" slang. To learn it I'd have a noggin to scrape (a hard task) that could moider my brains (disturb me greatly), especially on such a brief visit.

By noon I had stocked my camper van with food, supplies, and personal gear. Gas, oil, tires, battery—check. I was ready to head west, save for one parting rite. Mile 0 on the Trans-Canada stands at Confederation Building in midtown, but I drove to the harbor and parked on Water Street, the oldest public way in North America. The dockside air smelled of brine and diesel oil; bright red and orange ships rode upon the

Linked by ferry routes, the Trans-Canada Highway winds for 1,290 miles through the weathered Atlantic Provinces. While dense forests here remained long unexplored, teeming fishing banks lured Europeans by the early 1500s. Control of the valuable codfish catch ignited the French and English struggle for the New World. Recently discovered offshore oil deposits promise new riches.

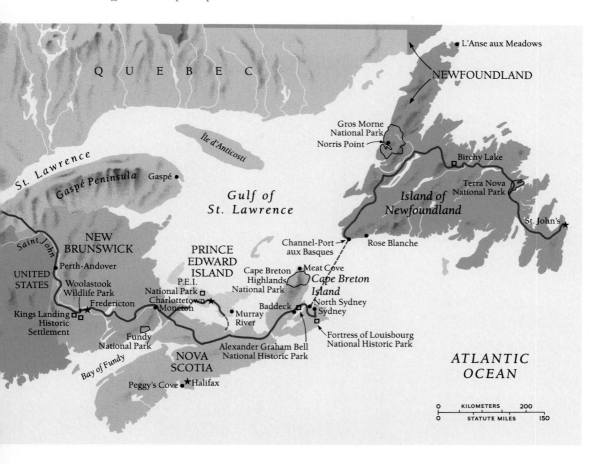

blue-green water. I scooped up a quart—make that a liter—of Atlantic Ocean and doused the back tires. Bon voyage.

The Trans-Canada runs 565 miles across Newfoundland, a distance nearly equal to driving from Boston to Pittsburgh. Within that area lies Terra Nova National Park, where the road winds through dense boreal forest and along the rocky spines of sea coves. Completed in 1965, the highway provides inland access for many outport villages, long isolated and named like so many fishing boats: Hearts Delight, Blow Me Down, Witless Bay. Because 90 percent of the population lives in coastal towns, the island

interior remains wilderness, a haven for moose and woodland caribou.

On a gray rain-spitting day, moments of sun between slanting showers, I had the road to myself. Miles went by, a smooth flow of time through rough terrain. Great blunt-edged hills rose and fell; trees gave way to broad lakes lashed with foam. I slipped a tape into the van's player and sank into the tranced mood of motion. Passing road stripes blurred with the sweep of wipers, the singing hiss of wet tires. . . . The hard rattle of sleet startled me. Soon I was hunting for a campground in heavy, wet snow— bizarre for early June. *(Continued on page 22)*

Newfoundland's past echoes on Signal Hill, a 500-foot promontory guarding the port of St. John's. The musket drill reenacts those of the island's 19th-century British garrison. Until a bare majority of Newfoundlanders voted to join Canada in 1949, St. John's stood as the capital of Britain's oldest colony.

*Fishermen haul up their net from the rocky ocean floor off Newfoundland,
whose waters annually yield more than a billion pounds of cod and other fish.
Generations of islanders such as David Howlett (opposite, top) and his uncle,
Jack Howlett, continue a tradition sparked by explorer John Cabot's enticing
reports in 1497 of waters "swarming with fish." Though mining and timbering
provide needed jobs, most Newfoundlanders still turn to the sea.*

Flanked by towering granite, a tour boat takes sightseers up Western Brook Pond, a freshwater gorge in Gros Morne National Park on the western shore of Newfoundland. Carved by glaciers and fed by streams spilling over 2,000-foot cliffs, the sinuous canyon (right) winds for ten miles, from the Long Range Mountains to the coastal plain on the Gulf of St. Lawrence. In places, Gros Morne reveals rock from deep within the earth's mantle — one of few areas where such rock lies well exposed.

My hosts at Birchy Lake, Michelle Collins and Chris Etheridge, were glad to see one guest emerge out of the night's freak weather. Both students, they had come from distant towns for their summer jobs—which suggested just how tough things were in Newfoundland, where unemployment is nearly 20 percent. Once almost entirely dependent on fishing, the province is now hoping to develop new resources, such as offshore oil. "But oil out there won't help Newfoundland that much," Chris remarked. "Jobs and money have a way of going scarce here."

Even so, neither of them planned to leave the island. Over bowls of steaming homemade soup and fresh-baked bread, they spoke proudly of families who cling to their ways, whatever outsiders may think. "You'll hear a lot of Newfie jokes in Canada," Chris said, "that make us sound backward. We're survivors; not many could last here as long as we have." I heard that persistence in the soft burr of their words, hummed like a Celtic tune. When I left the next day, Michelle wished me a good journey: "You've no' got so far to go now, right?"

On the western coast I found the tree-stunted, ice-gouged world of Gros Morne National Park, where glaciers have carved long, narrow lakes that reach for the sea like grasping fingers. These "ponds" resemble fjords, with steep cliffsides and deep V-shaped bottoms, but their water is fresh. "It comes from snowmelt above," park interpreter Jeff Anderson explained, "and passes through just a few outlets. The flow is extremely slow, which presents a high risk for pollution."

In this pristine world I could barely imagine problems, until my trail through Gros Morne joined that of Peter Ursel and Angela Murray. Together we hiked through upland swamps and meadows to the mouth of Western Brook Pond. A doctor and a nurse, they were serving as medical residents in the nearby village of Norris Point. Both spoke of the hardships of outport

life—poverty, disease, isolation. But Peter recalled that only a few nights ago much of Norris Point turned out at high tide to gather capelin, small fish that resemble smelt.

"We rolled up our pants and waded into the surf with plastic bags," he said. "The fish were spawning like mad, two males on either side of a female, and making a flurry in the water. People were laughing and shouting like little kids, and we stayed up for hours." I heard some nostalgia in his tone, for he and Angela were soon leaving. "I told my landlord I won't miss the winters here. He said, 'Oh my son, you come back here in July and you'll call Newfoundland home.'"

I made a night crossing to Nova Scotia, a six-hour trip across the Gulf of St. Lawrence on a Canadian National Marine auto-ferry. These broad-beamed vessels prime the Atlantic Provinces' arterial system, pumping a steady flow of traffic between the four provinces. My fellow passengers quickly dispersed into cabins or bedded down with sleeping bags on the lounge floor. All through the night a gull flew beside our boat, probably hoping for kitchen scraps. At 5:30 I went for coffee, but the steward shrugged off my money: "Have a wake-up, on the hoose."

Nova Scotia consists of two landmasses, a southern peninsula shaped like a hatchet—the blade striking New Brunswick—and, to the north, Cape Breton, an island hollowed by intruding saltwater lakes and channels. The place-names shift from French to English and Scottish, reflecting waves of strife that once swept the land. I came ashore at Cape Breton and took a brief detour back in time, going southeast beyond the steel mills at Sydney to reach Louisbourg, a quiet fishing harbor. Two miles down the road stands the Fortress of Louisbourg, where the time is always the summer of 1744. "Fortress" means a fortified town, almost 30

FOLLOWING PAGES: *Clinging to a rocky hillside, the fishing village of Rose Blanche faces seaward in western Newfoundland. Place-names here reveal that the French were first to settle this coast. Ninety percent of Newfoundlanders still live in coastal towns. A wilderness of forest and lake cloaks the interior of the island.*

acres of houses, shops, and barns surrounded by thick stone walls and guarded by musket-bearing sentries. They challenged me with menacing scowls and a curt burst of French: "Halt! State your business! Proceed!" But as I passed one picket, he winked and lapsed into English: "How's it going?" Inside I walked the streets of an 18th-century port, where France had once hoped to win control of the Maritimes.

In earlier days both French and British settlers lived quietly in Nova Scotia, only to be swept into their nations' colonial war over Canada. Louisbourg rose—and quickly failed, for it was too exposed to harsh weather and British attacks. Now a restored fortress stands in its place, as a national historic park. Its fortunes seem secure, since more than 150,000 tourists visit every summer. Scott and Lindsay Flammer came all the way from California; I found them happily dining at the tavern on pea soup, cod, and turnips. "We wanted something different for our honeymoon," said Scott, "and we sure got it!"

Together we poked around the fortress, pausing to talk with costumed guides about the lives they represented. We met soldiers and cooks, a grande dame decked in ballroom finery, a priest on his way to Mass. The place was less a museum than a lively, bustling village, full of blooming gardens and rooms to be dusted, bread baking and salted cod drying on outdoor racks. And outside the walls a pack of red foxes, in charge of mouse patrol.

In the town of Louisbourg I stayed at one of its several bed-and-breakfast homes. My hostess was Mrs. Greta Cross, bright-eyed and energetic at 72 years. A retired schoolteacher, she now sits on the town council, compiles local history, and spreads goodwill for Nova Scotia: "Lordy, this work keeps me busy. The house is full from May to November, and I've had guests from every province—plus 13 foreign countries." She bustled about her sunny kitchen: "Oh, it's a fair day. It speaks for a fine tomorrow, as well."

Breakfast was heaps of scrambled eggs, oatcakes, and fresh tomato slices. "You like the rhubarb jam? I never know if people will. More tea? Juice?" I was being grandmothered to a fare-thee-well. Over tea we talked about her latest project: "I'm studying to be a volunteer guide at the fortress. We have lectures and readings on the 1740 period—and tests! Oh, but the place is a boon to this area: There are over a hundred jobs out there. And many of the park's builders were ex-coal miners from the shut-down mines in Glace Bay. They learned skilled trades, and some today run their own businesses."

Loaded with apples, oatcakes . . . and a jar of rhubarb jam, I returned to the Trans-Canada and drove west. Soon I left a world of trim villages and cultivated fields to reach the Cabot Trail, a 184-mile loop through the Cape Breton Highlands. Considered one of the most scenic drives in North America, the Cabot Trail skirts rocky headlands that grip the sea with rounded paws. The thick forest cover was a painting in progress, dark streaks of spruce with daubs of young maple.

While the highlands are a playground for many summer visitors, I passed up beaches and golf courses to head farther north and meet some year-round residents. At the far end of Cape Breton a dirt road led me through hairpin turns to a village with the intriguing name of Meat Cove. The place has a reputation as standoffish, no doubt owing to its secluded location. But a welcome sign hung at The Meat Cove Pottery, and Dora Petronzio gave me a friendly greeting: "C'mon out back. I'm in the middle of glazing."

Her six-year-old, Nicholai, was busy at the pottery wheel, mauling a hapless piece of clay. "That boy has a mind of his own," she said. "He only learns the hard way." "Now I'm going to make a *bigger* one," he announced, holding up a lumpy doughnut. As Dora dipped pitchers in an oily red glaze, she talked about her chosen country. "I grew up in *(Continued on page 32)*

23

Sweeping by cliffs and coves, the Cabot Trail climbs through Nova Scotia's Cape Breton Highlands National Park on its scenic 184-mile route. Inland, the road penetrates a boggy wilderness of high plateau, where moose, bear, and bobcat range. Cape Breton Island's deep valleys and wind-ruffled lakes reminding them of home, waves of Scots immigrated here beginning in the 1790s. In North Sydney, young bagpipers keep the old music alive.

FOLLOWING PAGES: Raucous gulls break the stillness of a misty morning in Peggy's Cove, a rustic fishing village on Nova Scotia's southern coast. Painters and photographers outnumber fishermen nowadays in the rigorously preserved village. Nova Scotia's centuries-old fishing industry accounts for a full quarter of the national harvest, with lobsters and scallops dominating the catch.

Winter's hush enfolds Bras d'Or, a 450-square-mile salt lake on Cape Breton Island. From a workshop near his summer mansion, in the background, Alexander Graham Bell engineered a hydrofoil that hit 70 miles per hour on these waters in 1919. A national historic park in nearby Baddeck displays the hydrofoil and other Bell inventions, including his most famous—the telephone.

Kingston, upstate New York, and now have landed immigrant status in Canada." Why settle here? She nodded at her ocean view. "For the beauty and solitude, but it's changed a lot. We had 6,000 visitors at our shop last year, and many more came just to see the village."

Back on the Cabot Trail, I drove south along the sunset edge of Cape Breton through a silken afternoon light. The sea was calm, so flat that gulls sat down to float like ponded ducks. Shingled fishing shacks went by, brief paint strokes of blue, yellow, pink, green, red. The signs read Petit Étang and Belle-Marche, for I had entered a remnant of Acadia. That was the Maritime realm of early French settlers, whom

the British forcibly deported in the 1750s and '60s. Longfellow's *Evangeline* described their long, sad voyage to Virginia and Louisiana. Although most "Cajuns" remained there, some later resettled on Cape Breton. I passed the Acadian Motel, followed by Le Restaurant Evangeline.

The last stretch of Cabot Trail swung inland and led me past green fields and low vales, cottage towns called Margaree Forks, Finlayson, Baddeck. The Scottish names suited this scenery and so did the weather, as a blustery rain came in behind a southwest wind. Mist hung in the hills and fir trees, making ghostly, feathered shapes. I could see why so many Scots who left their highland tenant farms settled here in the 1790s. This country has the fens and lochs that recall north-western Scotland.

Especially the lochs, for I had come to the wide salt lakes that form an inland sea across lower Cape Breton. In 1885 a young Scottish inventor named Alexander Graham Bell spent a holiday in Baddeck and promptly fell in love with the broad waters of Bras d'Or Lake. After many visits he built "Beinn Bhreagh," a turreted house and workshop complex, where he developed an astounding array of farsighted ideas in medicine, aviation, and marine transport.

At Baddeck I spent some hours absorbing this story at Alexander Graham Bell National Historic Park, a large A-frame exhibition center overlooking Baddeck Bay. The modern structure resembles Bell's early flight designs, tested as huge tetrahedral kites. Visitors were queuing to shout messages over an early Bell telephone: "Mr. Watson, come quickly!" was a popular line. Outside, rain fell steadily into the lake, a test site for many of Bell's experiments. The winter ice became a launch site for Canada's first airplane; in summer Bell's hydrofoils skimmed the water at 70 miles per hour.

A much slower boat ride carried me to Prince Edward Island. After crossing the Canso Causeway from Cape Breton to mainland Nova Scotia, I caught a ferry at the town of Caribou for the 14-mile ride to Canada's smallest province. About the size of Delaware, Prince Edward Island is a 140-mile-long crescent tucked behind Nova Scotia and New Brunswick in the Gulf of St. Lawrence. Sheltered from North Atlantic storms, the island has a warm climate and sandy soil, where farming and tourism prosper. Wanting to sample both, I turned off the Trans-Canada—which hugs the south coast for 71 miles—and began a looping circuit along country roads.

Over gentle swells of field and forest, I passed small, narrow farms, each separated by hedgerow borders or painted fences. The houses wore Victorian dress: many-gabled roofs and gingerbread trim, with lines of wash on the Monday breeze. A tidy and clipped farmscape, it favored row crops of tobacco and potatoes, lush meadows dotted with bright dandelions. Prince Edward had a familiar look, but its own modest scale: "My father used to say this place was like a tiny bit of England that had broken off and drifted over here," said Jean Shumate.

I had come to the town of Murray River, population 400, and stopped at a shop called the Toy Factory. Jean introduced me to her husband, Al, a jovial white-bearded figure. "When he wears a red cap at Christmas," Jean laughed, "the kids think they've seen the real McCoy!" Al was turning out small wooden cars, trucks, and planes, the kind that Santa delivered back in 1948. That year Al first visited Prince Edward: "It was like stepping back 50 years to see those dirt roads and gabled houses. People would lean out from their chairs to watch you go by."

In 1968 he and Jean retired from the States to a family property on Prince Edward. "Woodwork began as a hobby, just to make gifts for the local kids. First I copied from books, then drew my own patterns. Now we sell toys at five shops on the island, and all across the country." Crafts are a major cottage industry in Canada, closely tied to tourism and its souvenir sales. "I organized a craft cooperative in Murray River, and twice a year we display items at the Toronto Gift Show, Canada's largest wholesale exhibition."

Al takes a bemused view of this career, for which he had no background: "I retired from the U.S. Army Field Band, where I was an arranger and conductor." Amid the wood shavings and glue pots I noted a citation from the French Foreign Legion. "In '43 I was a pistol instructor for them in North Africa, on loan from British army intelligence." He saw my expectant look. "Spy work is duller than you think. Mostly it's waiting for things to happen." Life here once was just as quiet: "In '48 I met people who had never gone off-island. At our church in Summerside, some kids had never seen Charlottetown." The towns lie 43 miles apart.

In Charlottetown I found a ceremony under way at Province House, as ranks of soldiers and a military band paraded in the street. No one stopped to watch but me, a snoop with clicking cameras. Royal Mounties in scarlet tunics and tall boots snapped to attention as a top-hatted ·dignitary appeared. "The lieutenant governor," a spectator told me, "Queen's representative in Prince Edward." This chap had sidled up while I was shooting pictures. He was dressed casually, but his cap wore a medallion: Royal Canadian Mounted Police.

Canadian government is an odd mix of federal power and colonial sentiment. Inside Province House—a historic site still used by the provincial legislature—is a chamber known as "The Birthplace of Canada." The room features a large table for legislators. Real authority sits with the provincial premier, his cabinet ministers, and members of the current majority party—a system similar to that of Canada's national government. At the table's corners stand tall wicker baskets, for discarded plans and papers. In 1864, delegates from the Maritime colonies met here to discuss a possible union. They chucked that idea when Canada West and East (today's Ontario and Quebec) pushed for a larger alliance. Together, the "Fathers of Confederation" assembled the British North America Act, which united four colonies as provinces in a Dominion of Canada. Proclaimed on July 1, 1867, the new nation was independent but still a British monarchy; this status endures even since adoption of a new constitution in 1982.

From Charlottetown I drove north across a rolling landscape of brick-red hills draped with a cloak of green. Near the coast a pale sugary sand was sifting across the road as I entered Prince Edward Island National Park. In early June the 304 campsites at Cavendish Beach were mostly empty, but the gatekeeper was expecting crowds: "After two or three weeks we'll be full most nights till September. People answer daily roll calls just to get a site." He handed me leaflets on the piping plover, an endangered shorebird. "We've got 15 to 20 nesting pairs left, and the world total is down to a thousand pairs."

After supper in a sheltering spruce grove, I took a long walk on Cavendish Beach. The tide was out, but offshore winds had raised great wide combers, olive green and lashed with froth. Gulls hung on the breezes, waiting to dip and glide along a promising wave. The sand here was a glossy white, lit by sunrays lancing down through scattered dark clouds. I was examining a washed-up lobster trap when Henk and Ann Van't Slot appeared on the horizon. At a distance they seemed young, walking arm in arm with matched strides. Close up, I met a trim, handsome couple in their mid-50s, dressed in bright jogging suits.

"We like to travel off season," Henk remarked, "when everyone else is home." Their home is Ontario, where Henk works as an engineer. Born in the Netherlands, the Van't Slots spent years of residence abroad after immigrating to Canada in the 1950s. "The States and Canada are the prettiest, healthiest countries we've seen," said Ann, "just right for raising families." Themselves the picture of robust health, they stood for a long while talking of children and travel, the joys of exploring Maya ruins. And what of careers? "When you get to be our age," Henk said, taking a poke in the ribs from Ann, "time becomes a lot more precious than money."

Time spun gold for Lucy Maud Montgomery, whose book *(Continued on page 42)*

Young fishermen bait their hook in front of storage lockers in Northport on Prince Edward Island. Anglers can fish for trout, salmon, and perch in fresh water and for cod, mackerel, and bluefin tuna in salt water. Some 60 wooden lighthouses dot Prince Edward, such as the one at North Rustico (left).

FOLLOWING PAGES: Strollers roam Cavendish Beach in Prince Edward Island National Park, 25 miles of dunes, cliffs, marshes, and ponds—and some of Canada's finest and most popular swimming beaches. Shielded from Atlantic storms by Nova Scotia and New Brunswick, the island enjoys a mild climate.

Orphaned month-old moose gambols with gamekeeper Scott Gordon at Woolastook Wildlife Park, a private reserve in central New Brunswick. At right, Scott feeds the calf while his daughter Heather looks on. Although the female moose has started to browse, Scott will continue to bottle-feed it for another three months. Woolastook's nursery rescues motherless moose, caribou, bear cubs, mink kits, and other creatures—to the delight

BOB SACHA (BOTH)

of visitors and campers at the park. New Brunswick's dense woodlands—an evergreen darkness brightened by birch and maple—abound with wildlife. Forestry has long been important here, with shipbuilders prizing the province's tall pines for masts since the 1600s.

Anne of Green Gables brought lasting fame to a farm near Cavendish Beach. Next morning I visited Green Gables, a white two-story house with green trim that sits on the edge of a golf course. Cars would drive up, deposit wives and daughters at the house, then carry stalwart males onward to the links. Montgomery's novel has sold millions of copies since its publication in 1908, and many of its devotees are women. One notable exception was Mark Twain, a cigar-smoking man of billiards and golf who praised the book as "the sweetest creation of child life yet written."

Inside Green Gables I stepped into a plain, severely clean farmhouse that Maud Montgomery often visited in childhood. An orphan reared by grandparents, she imagined this cousins' home as a refuge for young Anne Shirley, her redheaded, spunky dreamer who "never belonged to anybody—not really."

That detachment marked Maud Montgomery's life as well, for she worked several years as a teacher and writer before marrying a minister, and he never subdued her freethinking cast of mind. She accepted the role of parish wife and raised two sons, but kept to her writing—more than a dozen novels, places to escape and to remember "the good red earth" of Prince Edward.

Upstairs I heard laughter in the next room, from three visitors in their 20s. Richard Levangie and Thom Ward were playing mock guides for the benefit of their friend Kumiko Azetsu: "Oh, now this is Anne's famous bedroom. There's her bed and lace curtains, but of course the highlight here is her wash basin!" They were obviously not literary chaps, nor just pursuing an imaginary girl. Kumiko laughed at their sallies with a toss of smooth, black hair. She had come a long way to the Maritimes to study for a doctorate in science,

Boats floating off Alma, New Brunswick (opposite), sit stranded at low tide (below)—the result of earth's greatest tidal swing, in the Bay of Fundy. Tides vary more than 40 feet at Alma, near the headquarters of Fundy National Park. Most forceful during full or new spring moons, such tides can create great whirlpools and roll back rivers.

and she was nobody's fool: "Maud Montgomery's novels are very popular in Japan," she told me. "Parents think girls won't learn anything bad from them . . . like disrespect."

A short spin to the south brought me to New Glasgow, the sort of village that grows up around a crossroads and general store. "I ran a general store in the area 30 years ago," Ralph Dickieson said, "and visitors would stop to ask where they could buy fresh lobster in summer. So in June of 1958 the Junior Farmers put on a family-style supper at the church. We served less than a hundred that day; $2.25 for a whole lobster with rolls, salad, and cake or pie." Since then the lobster supper has become a summer industry for dozens of island villages. Ralph now runs nightly suppers from a large dining hall; a hundred cooks and servers handle more than 75,000 meals a season. He pats an ample middle: "Sure,

I enjoy lobster; ate a half dozen just last week."

He took me on a tour of the hall, which in an hour would be jammed with 550 hungry patrons. The kitchen was steamy with boiling pots and racks of cooling apple pie. "Pretty near everything served comes from the island, right down to cabbage for the coleslaw. We store the live lobsters in a saltwater pound, since fishing season is over during our peak demand." He opened a cold storage room, triple-tier tanks that held about 10,000 dark-clawed, twiddly lobsters in 40° circulating seawater. "I built this system out of ignorance," Ralph smiled, "but it's made to last."

One last brief ferry ride carried me to mainland New Brunswick, where the Maritimes begin to merge with French Canada. New Brunswick has a 1,400-mile coastline and a forested interior that sweeps west to reach Maine and Quebec.

One-third of the citizens descend from Acadians; hence the province has a large French-speaking population. Driving the Trans-Canada toward Moncton, I passed fieldstone houses with curved eaves, a classic French country style. A radio announcer was giving scores for "le Shee-caw-goh White Sox" as I turned south along the Petitcodiac River to head for the Bay of Fundy.

Twice a day this region faces the world's greatest tidal changes. As the sun and moon tug steadily at a turning earth, oceans respond in 12-hour cycles of rise and fall. Along most shores the change is slight and gradual, but the Bay of Fundy waters sweep up and down a long, tapering funnel. Sea levels swiftly drop 30 to 50 feet, then climb again as the bay refills. Pulled by gravity, the waters seem to defy its laws. Great whirlpools spin, long smooth waves enter rivers and run upstream, reversing rapids and falls. This tidal "bore," an old Norse word, is anything but boring. In Moncton, crowds gather at Bore Park on summer evenings to see the floodlit wave roll by.

I camped that night at Fundy National Park and next morning went out to explore low tide. Herring Cove, brimful last evening, was now a half-mile plain of drying gravel, streaked with shallow pools. The stones were cobble-size, rounded by a million tides into oval shapes of veined color: black, white, jade green, bright orange, and red. A mist was rising off the bay, where two lobster boats dipped and tossed on the lapping waves. Not much human life in sight, but on the return trail I walked through woods and meadows bursting from late spring into summer. Ferns and wildflowers crowded together, while ravens croaked and squabbled among green raspberries. Beneath an apple tree in bloom rested a quiet pair, one doe with her petal-dotted fawn.

A hundred miles west I met a baby moose, cradled in the arms of Scott Gordon. "I call her Chocolate, for her color," he said. "She's just 22 days old now and thinks I'm her mama." A tall, muscular father of two daughters, Scott manages Woolastook Wildlife Park, the Maritimes' largest private reserve of native animals. He walked me around the park's attractive, well-kept grounds, where caribou and moose graze in large enclosures. "An adult moose needs at least ten acres of room to tolerate captivity," he said. "Yogi out there, he's a full-grown bull at 900 pounds. We'll mate him with Chocolate in a couple of years."

Right now she had eyes only for Scott. When he set her down she instantly bawled and tottered stiffly after him. The old joke holds that a moose is an animal designed by a committee. With her stiff, wide-sprung legs and drooping snout, Chocolate was a comical, gangly bundle of 85 pounds. Still, she had a soft dark coat and large brown eyes. Scott held her bottle, a half-gallon nippled jug, which she attacked with rapture. "Like many of our animals, she was found alone in the woods, about starved. On this formula she's gained weight fast, and now she's learning to browse." After the meal came her daily jog, following Scott's lead for a quick mile.

Elsewhere in the park, Scott and I looked in on a Maritime menagerie of gray squirrels and white porcupines, wily timber wolves and oafish bears. They generally came in pairs, as on Noah's ark, and many had nicknames: Grumpy, Wimpy, Bubu. One silver fox went into conniptions at the sight of Scott, rolling on its back with a whining bark: "That's Foxy Loxy; she wants her tummy rubbed. Think you're a dog, don't you, girl?" Two cats with no such confusion were Canada lynx, which hissed and growled at my approach. "Lynx love to growl," warned Scott, "and they don't just promise trouble."

Later we talked about the expenses of this business. "First there's the cost of gathering a collection, plus food and medicine. I do most of the health care, since vets don't want to vaccinate skunks." As he talked, school buses were pulling into the parking lot. "We always invite school groups in June. Once they get through the kids, the animals are broken in for summer."

Along the western side of New Brunswick, the Trans-Canada turns north and follows the meandering course of the Saint John River. Although the river is only 418 miles long, it acquires volume by draining the great North Woods watershed; hundreds of streams course from the forested wilds of Maine and Quebec. Above Fredericton I passed along the Saint John Valley, cut into broad sloping terraces by eons of slow river currents. The farms and towns along this route have a sturdy English spirit, for they were settled by British Loyalists who left America during the Revolution.

They remain loyal to their past, come hell or high water. When a dam on the river threatened to immerse many early buildings in 1963, people here moved the structures to a high bank downstream and built a restored village, Kings Landing Historical Settlement. I stopped there to walk around in the 1840s, a century after Louisbourg, through a town that measured Britain's growing dominance over Atlantic Canada. The houses were sturdy stone or frame structures, built for occupants with stout British names: Jones, Grant, Long, Fisher. On the mill pond stream a giant waterwheel turned slowly, driving a saw through logs with implacable force.

Wearing a long print frock, Margo Landry walked with me awhile and talked of her work as a costumed guide: "We have about a hundred on the staff, and everyone dresses according to the period. In July and August we have a 'visiting cousins' program; children get to dress up and join the village activities." I looked in at the school they attend, straight-backed benches that faced a somber slate: "Be humble: learn thyself to scan." The country chapel had a plain altar and

pulpit, decidedly Anglican. To Margo the Loyalists were English patriots, refugees from what she called "a civil war." But time had erased the old conflicts. Her future plans? "Graduate study in Grenoble—French is my second language."

Driving north, I followed the river along the edge of forested lands, which form 85 percent of New Brunswick and remain unsettled. Logs were stacked by the road, waiting to go to lumber towns where the air had the sharp, sweet smell of freshly cut wood. The trees were mixed species, growing together in brotherly confusion, but stacked by loggers into piles of conifer and broadleaf—the softwood bound for pulp and paper, hardwood for construction or fuel. In this land of the maple-leaf flag, I was finally seeing great stands of maple. That should mean maple syrup, I thought, and pulled into Perth-Andover for dinner.

In York's Dining Room, Bonni St. Thomas came to my table and recited the evening menu: "Today we have lobster, steak, scallops, rainbow trout, roast chicken, roast duck, southern-fried chicken, home-cured smoked pork chop served with pineapple, fried salmon steak, and Alaska king crab legs." I started to reply, but she wasn't done. "Your dinner comes with juice, salad, home-made bread, biscuits, a side order of a small entrée, dessert, and beverage." She poured me a glass of water and smiled: "Would you care to order now?"

York's does not serve such light fare every day; it will add roast beef, ham, and turkey to the entrées and offer baskets of date or oatmeal bread, along with corn fritters in maple syrup. An early summer dish is steamed fiddleheads, coiled fern tips that taste a bit like asparagus. In recent years York's has gained a wide reputation from serving Trans-Canada tour buses and two nearby air bases. Customers have carried the fame worldwide. "We've had guests from Alaska, Saudi Arabia, Australia," said Bonni. "Why, we've even had folks from Newfoundland!"

Challenging the frigid St. Lawrence River, competing teams heave ice canoes over shifting floes as they race between Quebec City and Lévis on the opposite shore. This annual event climaxes Winter Carnival, one of French Canada's enduring traditions. The race recalls the days when farmers on river islands relied on steel-reinforced canoes for travel during the months when ice clogs the St. Lawrence.

INTO

FRENCH CANADA

Quebec

A life on the road is not always glamorous, I decided, as the stranger next to me began to scrub his teeth—the set held firmly in his hand. Campgrounds had begun to fill up with vacationers, for I had left behind spring and entered the brief, warm Canadian summer. The growing frequency of French signs and conversations told me I was also approaching Quebec, heart of French Canada. On the water taps, "C" no longer meant Cold but *Chaud*, Hot. Some mornings that made little difference, if I lost the race for the showers.

Camping had settled down into a semigypsy life. The van was now a home of sorts, free of mail and bills to pay, no gutters to clean or lawns to cut; just a place to cook and sleep, a sunny spot to write with music playing, while air spilled in the windows. I found plenty of campgrounds along the Trans-Canada, ranging from large national parks to private courts. Nearly all were clean, cheap, and run by cordial hosts. One of every ten Canadians earns a living from tourism, an industry carefully governed by provincial regulations.

Since I was traveling alone, on many evenings I walked around and met the neighbors. Couples would be setting up tents and stoves, while their kids ran off to fetch water. The families ate at picnic tables, wearing sweaters against cool nights. Somewhere an ax was always thunking into wood, and after dark the open fires flared. Fireside talk replaced the glowing Tube, except for some diehards in motor homes. Nearly every conversation began with license plates: "You're a long way from Washington, D.C." "I'm really from New Jersey." "Oh . . . do you know Bruce Springsteen?"

The dominance of U.S. culture troubles many Canadians, but Quebecois have a greater concern over the English language. Although one-fourth of Canada speaks French, enough to justify a bilingual nation, its Francophones are not widely distributed: 85 percent of them live in Quebec Province along a 150-mile-wide corridor centered in the St. Lawrence River Valley. Such is the remnant of New France, part of a trading empire that once claimed more than half the North American continent—from the Maritimes to the Rockies and Louisiana. But pride in a Gallic heritage still abides in Quebec, where every license plate bears the provincial motto: *Je me souviens,* I remember.

Crossing the border, I got out my French phrase books and kept them close at hand. The signs going by were not bilingual, though I could easily translate *Bar-à-go-go* and *Danseuses nues,* especially with their curvaceous neon forms. *Deux Prochaines Sorties* was more opaque: the next two exits ahead. I passed swiftly through woodlands and small towns (one with the jolly name of St-Louis-du-Ha! Ha!) to reach the St. Lawrence River, *fleuve St-Laurent.* In French, a small river is *rivière,* a grand one *fleuve;* the St. Lawrence earns that rank from its 800-mile length and its massive volume, greatest among Canadian rivers.

From a hill above the town of Rivière-du-Loup, I looked across a 12-mile width of St. Lawrence, and downstream this gap only spread as river rolled on to sea. Here the water was brackish, a mix of fresh and salt that encouraged whales and marine fish to come far inland and feed. When Jacques Cartier sailed up the river in 1535, the story goes, great schools of codfish slowed his ship's progress. Today some fishing boats were out, dwarfed by ocean-bound freighters—and beyond, by the rising Laurentian Mountains, wrapped in a smoky blue haze.

For all its immensity, this broad vista only hinted at Quebec's size. Largest of the provinces, Quebec contains nearly 600,000 square miles, or one-sixth of the Canadian landmass. But nearly half of this area is an unpeopled wilderness, just forest and subarctic tundra reaching north to Hudson Bay. The north-south length of Quebec is 1,200 miles, a drive from Maine to Florida.

After skirting the lower end of the rugged Gaspé Peninsula, the Trans-Canada turns southwest into the St. Lawrence River Valley. Preserving the Gallic heritage of their forebears, 85 percent of Canada's Francophones live along a narrow corridor centered in this valley. The highway here threads verdant countryside before reaching the province's capital, Quebec, and its largest city, Montreal.

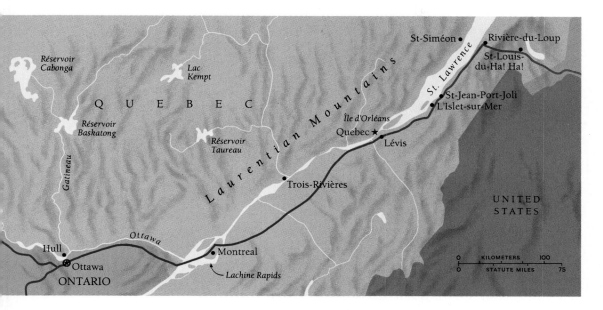

I was crossing the narrow end, from Maine to New York.

The Trans-Canada runs through the eastern towns of Bas-St-Laurent—lower St. Lawrence—remaining on high ground about a mile from the river. This wide four-lane expressway moves traffic rapidly upriver to Quebec City and Montreal, but I preferred a slower pace. Soon I turned onto Highway 132, a shoreline road that winds past fields and harbor towns, most with spired cathedrals. These villages grew up on *seigneuries,* 17th-century estates platted in narrow strips, each abutting the river. The *seigneur* rented land to his *habitants,* and everyone tithed to the church. New France had two capitals, Paris and Holy Rome.

"This is a little town; if I wash the windows everybody knows that. I make a Madonna of the Visitation for the Pope once, and so many people come to touch the figure that I have to clean it before sending to Rome." Benoi Deschênes smiled and swept some shavings to the floor. I had stopped at his riverside studio in St-Jean-Port-Joli, a village grown famous as a center for wood carving. For several hours I watched over his shoulder as he carved a new piece, a low-relief river scene for a retired fisherman. Benoi talked constantly as he worked, leaping through subjects while his hands slowly modeled the wooden slab.

"I carve on basswood, butternut, pine, sometimes exotics like mahogany, but they must have no cracks or knots and age in the open air. Two years is enough, but I prefer five to ten. Basswood is the easiest to work, see?" He pushed with a gouge and strips came away like curls of butter. "But the tool is sharp; this is dangerous." One of his fingers was blunted from an old accident. "Each knife has a name: flat or curved fishtail, deep gouge, backbent gouge; each for a different job." Did carvers pass on their tools? "No, it's like a toothpick; you can't use somebody else's."

The flourishing of wood carving in St-Jean-Port-Joli began around 1930, when churches sought to replace old plaster statues, mainly imports from Europe. Carving became a winter trade for local farmers and sailors, families named Bourgault, Guay, Gaudreau. Benoi is the first Deschênes to carve, but his name is propitious: "It means oak trees . . . oak is too hard to carve by hand, though, and power tools lose the artistic." The pursuit of that quality entails skill, patience, and generous patrons. "Some of my customers ask for perfection. I tell them perfection is not in the world, but I will try to do something you like."

They clearly do, for Benoi has a steady line of prizewinning commissions to his name, pieces that reflect his love of the Canadian past: voyageurs in a long bark canoe, the Fathers of the Confederation, a family gathering hay. "That's my father and brothers. In my family, we are 11 brothers and one sister. She is the princess, and we have a baseball and bowling team all together." Most of his models are friends or villagers, like a young fisherman: "He's a fellow with a good *barbe*—beard—and when it grew longer, I said 'Hey wonderful, I don't recognize you.' I use everybody; if not, you risk carving the same lumberjack over and over. I want to make portraits in wood, like a book of living people."

In his hands the gouge was turning a flat pencil sketch of boat and men into rounded figures with depth and shadow. "One hand is the power, the other the driver. I don't cut straight but twisting, to make it easier . . . if not, the hands will ache after eight hours." He fell silent during a difficult passage, bringing out the fine detail of ropes and wire. At last they seemed to stand free of the background, just the effect that he was after.

"Wood is so fragile it must be solidly connected. If I want to make fine, strong details, I go to bronze." But wood has grain and life; in time, its surface mellows to a golden patina. He gestured at a drawing: "My neighbor, 84 years old. When I work alone here, sometimes I'm tired and would like to go out.

Then I see him in his garden and I feel better."

That evening I camped a few miles upriver at L'Islet-sur-Mer, a village with a long maritime history. The camping spaces each bore names of former local boats. My berth was *Fabiola,* honoring an 81-ton vessel that sank with all its cargo in 1917. For a while I considered moving next door, to *Hope.* The life of St. Lawrence mariners is still a hard lot, for storms can swiftly lash the river into a whitecapped sea. Winter ice, fogs in all seasons; through such hazards the boatmen of L'Islet-sur-Mer sail on. And among its stone houses and flower gardens the village keeps a small riverside chapel with the inscription *Au Secours des Marins,* for the aid of our sailors.

I thought of security the next day while driving to Quebec City, once the military stronghold of New France. Near this provincial capital the river sharply contracts, forking around the great island of Orléans—a countryside of white cottages and strawberry fields—and thinning to a narrow gap at Cape Diamond, a stone promontory that rears more than 350 feet above the water. The flats below were an Indian camp when Cartier visited in 1535; by 1608 Samuel de Champlain had built a trading post there and was busy fighting Indians. Quebec City prospered, spread up and over its rocky heights, and during the 1700s became a walled fortress against repeated British efforts to breach the upper St. Lawrence.

Today the main assailant was a summer storm, which folded the city in deep roiling mist. By noon the skies had cleared as I walked down the Grande Allée past a monument inscribed "Je me souviens." Quebec is the town of I remember, and for me it awakens memories of many previous visits. Something about its narrow streets and gray stone walls, the old cannons that bristle in mock defense, breathes a touch of melancholy, not sad but brooding and stoic. The city has seen its hopes rise and fall; it faces every spring as a prelude to a long winter.

Nothing can turn back the winter season, so Quebec instead puts on a rousing good party. Every February the city holds Winter Carnival, a frostbite version of Mardi Gras. For two weeks, crowds of celebrators brave subzero cold and bitter winds to frolic in the snowy streets. Bands parade by, the musicians mittened and ruddy, while artists build colossal ice sculptures in a park on the Grande Allée. Down on the river, canoe teams race to cross the ice-clogged waters, cheered on by a throng of bundled, horn-tooting spectators. After Carnival they face the Lenten season—a time to pile logs on the fire, contemplate, and wait.

I was jostled out of these reflections by a large party of youngsters who brushed by me at the entrance to St-Louis Gate. A harried teacher scuttled after them: "Could you *please* remember that other people want to use the sidewalk?" Quebec City was full of visiting students, for whom this trip was a prelude to summer freedom. Dressed in bright red or blue uniforms, they shouted and raced along the town walls, whooping from ramparts and tumbling down grassy slopes. The walls stood up to these invaders, so I mounted to make a survey of my own.

From that elevation the city resembled a ship that had run aground on the high bluff of Cape Diamond. The old city, divided into *Haute-Ville* and *Basse-Ville,* Upper Town and Lower Town, was an angular bow pointing downriver, crowded with squat stone houses and crowned by the turreted bulk of Château Frontenac, a landmark hotel. Behind me rose modern Quebec City, the broad high-rise jumble where most residents work and live. Once a defensive bulwark, the town walls are now flanked by cafés and garden parks. Horse-drawn calèches offer circuits of Upper Town, but I followed several visitors on a wall promenade.

At Artillery Park I stopped to inspect a former arsenal and military barracks, reminders of old conflicts. For three centuries these buildings formed part of Quebec's military complex. At first they housed the armies of successive French and British regimes. Later they were the site of an ammunition factory. Today the buildings offer living history, as films and puppet shows reenact the past—always in French and English. The most popular exhibit is an 1808 model of the city, built to assist military strategists. Their life was not always grim, according to one barracks sign: "All brandy and wine drunk, with the exception of champagne, will be charged equally among those who partake."

I followed the walls past views of factories and cobbled streets to reach Château Frontenac, a hotel built by the Canadian Pacific Railway in 1893 in a grand medieval style. With its soaring brick walls and copper roofs, now aged to a pale blue-green, the Frontenac remains a busy center for visitors to Old Quebec. Amid the swirl of traffic, I noticed a young woman on her hands and knees. Alison McGain was carefully digging in the hotel grounds, removing layers of soil with a trowel and whisk broom. "Are you doing archaeology?" "Oh, in a modest way. These are guardhouse footings. If you want to see a full-scale dig, go around the château."

Alison directed me to the wide, planked boardwalk of Dufferin Terrace, which overlooks the St. Lawrence. Strollers here can survey one of the grandest views in North America, a panorama of river and countryside washed in miles of light and air. Today most visitors were gathered around a gaping hole in the boardwalk. Directly below, 20 laborers in overalls and hard hats were deep in the mud of 17th-century Quebec. The crew was excavating part of the southeast courtyard of the original Château St-Louis, home of the early governors of New France. Soon I met Monique Elie, a Parks Canada archaeologist who cheerfully invited me *(Continued on page 65)*

Carriage horses clip-clop through St-Louis Gate, in a section of the stone walls surrounding historic Quebec City. Begun in the early 1700s, the walls now divide Old Quebec—designated a UNESCO World Heritage Site in 1985—from the modern city. Above, visitors peruse local artwork in the open-air gallery along rue du Trésor. France Bégin (below) reaches for a bite of Pierre Giguère's lobster as they lunch at Aux Vieux Canons, one of Quebec's many outdoor cafés.

MAGGIE STEBER (ABOVE AND OPPOSITE)

Accordion music serenades strollers on narrow rue Petit-Champlain in Quebec's Lower Town. Springing up along the north bank of the St. Lawrence, Lower Town once cradled civilization in New France: Here Samuel de Champlain built his settlement, Habitation, in 1608. Green-turreted Château Frontenac (above) crowns Upper Town, part of the old city that rises above the river. Completed in 1893, this hotel remains one of Quebec's most famous landmarks. Separated from the Frontenac by a steep cliff, red-roofed Hôtel Chevalier, now a museum, dates from 1752.

Reigning as a major port and industrial center, Quebec City sits on a rocky promontory above the St. Lawrence. Sleek skyscrapers of the modern city tower beyond the Château Frontenac, at center. At left stretch the Plains of Abraham, marking the scene of the British victory over the French in 1759—an event that all but ended France's military presence in Canada.

Undaunted by the -20°F temperature, revelers clad in beach attire rub down with snow in a Winter Carnival ritual called Bain de neige. In the background stand the walls of the stately snow palace, built each year at the Place du Palais. Four weeks before the carnival, architects and artists began to fashion the structure from several hundred tons of snow. During the ten-day celebration, different groups serve breakfast around Quebec City. Above, early risers on the rue Ste-Thérèse queue up for a free western repast prepared by representatives of the Calgary Exhibition and Stampede. To decorate the city, both local and international artists sculpt snow creations, such as the party of silent observers at right.

to see the dig. "Take a hard hat," she advised, and I borrowed one with a nameplate: Lucie Giroux. The workers were mainly college students, about half of them women, and down in the excavation site they were lugging heavy loads of dirt and rock. Monique and I threaded our way around pools of standing water, trying not to slip on the wet clay and piles of debris. Over the racketing noise of a jackhammer, she explained the finds so far: "We can see the remains of a series of outbuildings that served the château. These walls were a greenhouse, a *glacière*—or icehouse—and privies. Also some drains, where the waste water went."

That may not sound like everyone's idea of discovery, but archaeology thrives on the trash of lost generations. "We have recovered several pieces of window glass, flowerpots, some dishes and bowls. In an ashpit, we found some kitchen refuse like bones and eggshells." Systematic excavation has also exposed the southeast bastion of Fort St-Louis, built in 1693. "Near the sally port, the outside door, we found a brick stove, built later for heating the greenhouse."

We turned and walked some distance under the boardwalk. "Over here is a British guardhouse, built in 1856." The guardhouse itself now faces blank stone walls, which support the walkway overhead. "We made part of last summer's excavation without opening up the boardwalk," Monique explained. "It was dark and wet under here, sometimes from beer or ice cream dripping down. The hard hats were essential!" This year's open dig had drawn great public interest, but the crew would close and cover it by fall. "Until then, Parks Canada has two guides on hand to answer questions. It's hard for us to shout back and forth with visitors, over the jackhammer."

In the quiet confines of a field lab, we looked at recovered artifacts: an earthenware plate with a willow pattern, some white crockery, part of a shovel. Was lab work exciting? "Not always, but it certainly is important,"

Monique answered, with a scientist's concern. Like all federal agencies, Parks Canada has its red tape and regulations, one of them being bilingualism. "But we don't speak much English till summer, when most of the tourists come to visit. Quebec is such a French city."

The descent to Lower Town dropped me some 200 feet, down the twisting turns of Côte de la Montagne street and its "Break-Neck Stairs" into Place Royale, the trading center of Old Quebec. Commerce is still brisk in this quarter, now restored to its appearance of the early 1700s. Today the shops sell chic clothing and jewelry; cafés hawk "la pizza" at gourmet prices. I gathered a sack lunch from an *épicerie* and ate in the sunny market square. A clown came by, leading troops of children. Some stopped to give pennies to a banjoist, who was playing folk tunes. Two couples sat nearby; one deep in talk, the other grimly silent. A parade of sorts was passing me, *tout ensemble.*

Someone has lived on this spot for at least 2,500 years. The little church at my back, Notre-Dame-des-Victoires, was built in 1688 on the site of Samuel de Champlain's original trading post, Habitation. Before the Frenchmen came, Indians of the Iroquoian nation had a settlement here, called Stadaconé, according to the French. Names were not fixed in the New World, nor were rights of property. When Cartier came ashore in 1535 he asked the Indians what they called this land. "Kanata" was their answer, meaning settlement, a town. And so arose Canada, the misnomer that became a nation.

I ascended to Upper Town, then climbed even higher on the Promenade des Gouverneurs, a half-mile walkway anchored to the cliffs. Below spread the St. Lawrence, crossed by wakes of river ferries and ocean-bound vessels. Behind me reared the hulking gray stone walls of the

Citadel, a fort built by the British and still guarded by troops wearing red coats and tall bearskins. Those members of the Royal 22nd Regiment troop the colors and change the guard, ceremonies that recall Buckingham Palace. Yet their motto is French, Je me souviens; for they are Canadian soldiers—defenders of France and England in two world wars.

Beyond the Citadel I came to the Plains of Abraham. For two centuries these broad, rolling fields atop Cape Diamond were Quebec City's natural defense, a backyard that provided clear views upriver. As long as the city guarded its downstream side, no enemy could scale the cliffs and make a rear attack. Not until September 13, 1759, the day that spelled the end of New France. In a Parks Canada kiosk, interpreter Nicolas St-Cyr spread out some charts to explain what happened. "The French had more soldiers, but the British sealed off the river with their warships." He pointed upriver. "At a small cove, the British found a path up the cliffs and climbed after dark. Three point-blank volleys in the morning, and it was all over in 20 minutes."

A geographer by training, Nicolas tends to see history in earthy terms. "Quebec took this site for granted, and why not? It's solid stone, a platform left after faults opened the river. There's no water source up here, no runoff streams to cut valley slopes. No one expected 5,000 troops to climb a single path." He paused to give some visitors directions: rest rooms here, shopping and cafés over there. No one asked about the battle, I noticed. He shrugged: "The Europeans do; over there, every farmer knows the history of his fields. Mostly I talk to school groups." From across the Plains of Abraham such a force was approaching, rowdy and shouting in English. "They're probably from Toronto—they get a bit wild when far from home."

In the late afternoon I returned back up the Grande Allée, going past restaurants now filling with dinner patrons. The posted menus were sleek and tempting—coq au vin, saumon avec crevettes—and the clients mainly English-speaking tourists, grateful advocates of French cooking. Turning onto rue Cartier, I found a different neighborhood: Quebecois shopping at the end of day, sniffing cheese and squeezing fruit, arguing prices—Alors, trop cher! (too much)—sitting in cafés to wine and dine with friends. I heard no English, and none was offered; even the body language was French, delivered in rapid gestures with une moue, a deep grimacing pout.

Back in the 1960s this town and province made loud rumbles for political separation from Canada. At issue were the rights of Francophones, who felt consigned to second-class status for their language. Since the adoption of national bilingualism in 1969, such resentments have gradually ebbed. Although costly, the policy has begun to bring together two cultures that may one day bury their old hostilities. Nature speaks "a various language," wrote the poet; why should not we? Someone on rue Cartier had hung out a promising sign, well before the nation's birthday on July 1: Bonne Fête, Canada.

Beyond Quebec City I drove along the north shore of the St. Lawrence on Route 138, Canada's oldest highway. Opened in 1734, Le Chemin du Roi, or King's Road, passes through old seigneuries, where farming still prevails. Summer was rushing onward; suddenly the fields were waving in long, deep grass, sprinkled with white and yellow daisies. Wildflowers always love a roadside, where they can spread and catch the sun. For miles I ran beside banks of buttercups and wild radish, sweet clover laced with morning glories. Probably poison ivy and goldenrod, too; all in haste to bloom before the frosts of early September.

In late afternoon I reached Montreal, a town that won't stop growing. Nearly three million

strong, the population of this city—Canada's second largest, after booming Toronto—centers on a 32-mile-long island bounded by fast-flowing rivers. Here the Ottawa ends its 790-mile run from northern Quebec and flows into the St. Lawrence. Its natural junction of waterways made the city into a great inland port, home of the early fur trade and later a gateway to western settlement. At this rendezvous point I finally met photographer George Mobley, after weeks of separate travel east and west.

Together we set out the next day for one of Montreal's surprises, a ride on white-water rapids within the city limits. Until the St. Lawrence Seaway opened in 1959, large boats could not navigate the infamous Lachine Rapids, a turbulent rock-strewn channel just below the rivers' confluence. Many lives ended at Lachine, as did many dreams of reaching China, *La Chine,* via this northwest passage. When Champlain faced the rapids in 1603, he beheld a discouraging barrier: "Never did I see such a wildly raging torrent of water." Today the torrent runs a bit more sedately, but you'd never guess that—to hear Jack Kowalski talk.

"Ladies and gentlemen, *mesdames et messieurs,* if you want to ride on the raging river but not get wet, then take the harbor cruise. This is the wet ride: You put on a rain suit, a hat and sandals; we're not the high fashion center of Montreal." The crowd giggled nervously and struggled into bright yellow slickers. A bilingual spieler, Jack kept up his patter with gags and songs. One client had never worn a sou'wester hat: "Hey, turn it around; you look like The Flying Nun." Then a group announcement, "Here's the most important part of the trip: how to save your own life. Keep the vest on tight; if you don't . . . you're not gonna make it!"

Soon that phrase became a running joke, as the 700-horsepower jet boat roared up Jack's "River of No Return." Along the way he kept us entertained on his bullhorn, an appropriate medium: "Folks, it's ten minutes till the rapids and we have something very important to discuss. No, not life insurance." A few chuckles arose. "I have to tell you that sometimes we encounter giant whirlpools. Haven't seen them today, but we're due. Don't worry, we won't get sucked under any, deeper than 15 or 20 feet." Open laughter now. "And if we do . . ." The boat chorused back, "We're not gonna make it!"

In fact, the rapids turned out to be a good ride. We swooped up and down over tall standing waves washed with foam. In French, whitecaps are sometimes called *saute moutons,* or jumping sheep, and at points the river looked like a rumpled, leaping flock of woollies—"the foaming fury," Jack called it, but then he insisted that the gulls were vultures: "They're getting hungry, too; we haven't fed them in a week." In an aside to me, he confided one truth about the ride: "It changes every time we go through; depends on how the waves are blowing up and moving." We skimmed by a swirling vortex and slid into a deep trough. Jack took his cue: "Here comes the meanest mother wave of them all, and if we don't stay straight. . . ."

With his cheeky manner and mixed heritage—"a Polish father and Welsh-Irish mother; you could say I've kissed the Blarney stone"—Jack seemed to typify the spirit of Montreal. Quebec City is slightly grave, sedate; Montreal hustles with the color and flair of an international port. A major hub for rail and air services, the city also receives nearly 4,000 ships a year from all the world's corners. In time the population has grown amazingly diverse, as immigrants arrive from Europe, Asia, and Africa to settle into local neighborhoods. About two-thirds of Montrealers speak French; the rest use English and assorted languages.

On an evening walk, George and I sampled

Jet boat guide Jack Kowalski briefs passengers as they speed toward Lachine Rapids south of Montreal. This stretch of the St. Lawrence, impassable in Cartier's day, foiled the search for a route to China.

FOLLOWING PAGES: Boats hug the pier at Montreal. Situated on the St. Lawrence Seaway, this inland port links the Great Lakes with the Atlantic Ocean.

the city's potpourri of sights and smells. Along a single block we passed from diesel exhaust to sautéed garlic, then a heady boutique cologne. Say, look at that couple in Disney masks—are those *real* tommy guns? "No, just plastic," the one dressed as Goofy told us. "We are from Théâtre Zoopsie, waiting to pick up our boss." The next bus rolled up, and our masked duo "kidnapped" one of the passengers. All three ran off together, apparently playacting without script— or audience, since few Montrealers gawked at this incident. George and I passed on to Chinatown, streets lined with *épiceries chinoises* selling Peking jelly, tiger balm, and shark fin soup.

Lines had formed at the pagoda-shaped cinema, for a kung fu double feature.

A light drizzle glistened on Old Montreal, once the town's thriving center of trade. The old banks and stores are now renovated bistros, still upscale but empty on a wet night. At an outdoor fruit stand, two clerks passed the time by building intricate pyramids of apples, grapes, and oranges. George praised their fruit, no doubt because it came from his native California. Shabbier goods dominated the *marché aux puces,* a flea market on the river docks, but the patrons seemed ready to haggle. Buying, selling, making deals; trading has gone on here for 350 years.

Hosannas of color and light greet parishioners awaiting a Saturday Mass in the Notre-Dame Basilica, Montreal's premier example of church architecture. American architect James O'Donnell completed the Gothic Revival basilica in 1829. The church's dazzling main altar displays elaborate wood carvings designed by Canadian architect Victor Bourgeau and French sculptor Bouriché.

Montreal is Amsterdam rolled into Paris, a town where burghers and bohemians have built a vibrant New World culture.

At noon the next day the sun was high and warm, and the streets began to jump with rhythmical sound. In the quarter along rue St-Denis, we found the Montreal International Jazz Festival well under way. An annual event, the festival brings together artists from several continents for ten days of performing, most of it free and outdoors. "Jazz" meant anything from Dixieland to rock, with plenty of blues and bossa nova thrown in. I had thought of jazz as a U.S. idiom, until I heard two Czechs on clarinet and sax uncork an old Charlie Parker tune. They took the melody out for a long stroll, improvising solos but ending on a chorus. *"Formidable!"* cheered the crowd.

At least half my fun was watching this festival audience. Mellowed by the sun—and ample libation—people picked up the beat with toes and fingers, or just little nods of the head. A toddler kept time by whapping his blue balloon; a woman in a wheelchair tapped on her armrests. No one stayed put; roving on foot or bike was all part of the day's freedom. They sat in the streets or listened from windows, gossiped over drinks and shared ice-cream cones. One enterprising biker was collecting cans and bottles for the deposit money; another handed out leaflets touting his handmade sandals. The street performers were out in force: jugglers and quick-sketch artists, a one-man band playing ricky-tick rags. All we need is a fire-eater, I thought, and then I saw the mime.

In the shade of a sycamore tree, Marin O'Neil was quietly transforming himself into Count Magibaba, a lean and elegant figure in black with a snow-white mask for a face. He was adding his eye marks, a red heart and blue star, but had not yet assumed the veil of silence. "My act is mime and magic; last year I did fixed pose, like a robot, and only moved when people put money in the hat. Now I use the magic to create a focus, make them wonder what's coming next."

He set up a tripod and assembled some scarves, sponge balls, and the stuff of sundry illusions. "In the streets you have to improvise, go with the crowd that gathers. None of my shows are the same." A youngster approached and shyly asked for the Count's autograph. He complied, after plucking a ball or two from the astonished boy's ears.

Marin lifted a top hat and slowly settled it on his head, making several strong grimaces. I had the feeling that he was dissolving into Magibaba. "He has a Spanish look, serious but with an eye for girls. His life story isn't all there yet, but I'm working on it." Is he a friend? "A partner—he makes me wear long hair for a Latin look, and I need him to make the magic work." Those were his last words to me. Five minutes later, Count Magibaba had a crowd of a hundred persons—all ages, races, and national origins—wholly transfixed, as hushed as his performance with cards and scarves.

Something of that mood descended on me at the end of day, as I heard some Canadians play a set of deep Mississippi blues. It was music from the South's old father of waters, played on the banks of a north-flowing river, in a town that calls fried chicken *poulet frit,* by a band from Saskatchewan. But how they played! As darkness fell, the crowd began to seethe and heave; even the corner traffic lights pulsed in 4/4 time.

On a long harmonica solo, one man took the music and made it into a soulful ride, first as a chugging train, then a roaring wind, until the sound belled upward, sailing beyond the mansard roofs and church steeples into the wide night sky. We called for encores, but the band said it was time to go: *"Merci,* Montreal. . . . Thanks a million, folks. . . . *Au revoir,* Quebec!"

Mime Marin O'Neil, in character as Count Magibaba, charms a young fan during Montreal's annual International Jazz Festival—when music fills the streets for ten days near the beginning of July. Several blocks of rue St-Denis are closed to traffic, allowing groups to perform in the bustling Latin Quarter (below). Taking a break from the festivities, a couple shares an ice cream cone.

Flashing a red garter and a bright smile, Johanne Leblanc cancans down the runway at a fashion show in Montreal, the haute couture center of French Canada. This show, a charity benefit for the handicapped, featured fashions from 1900 to the year 2000. On the rue Bonsecours, fashion designer Edwin Birch (below) warms model Ginette Jarret with a bear hug. Model Myriam Brulotte wears a vivid Mexican print designed by Birch.

FOLLOWING PAGES: Birch designs, worn by models Brulotte and Jarret, rival a banner celebrating Canadian themes in Maison Alcan, headquarters of Alcan Aluminium Ltd. Maison Alcan combines a modern office structure with shops and restaurants housed in adjoining renovated buildings—a sample of Montreal's efforts to preserve a vital urban core.

Canada Day throngs rim the east lawn of Ottawa's Parliament Hill during a ceremonial changing of the guard on the national birthday, July 1. This Gothic home of the federal legislature perches on a bluff above the Ottawa River, one of countless rivers and lakes in Ontario—whose name comes from an Iroquoian word for "the shining waters."

SHINING WATERS

Ontario

Beyond Montreal the Trans-Canada slips through a little angled corner of Quebec and then quietly enters Ontario. The border is just a survey line drawn across flat lowlands that reminded me of Illinois, my boyhood home. Silos marked the horizon, also fringes of oak and ash edging green fields. Wild mustard bloomed along the roadside, and the summer air shimmered with rising heat. But I saw one difference: Corn was just shin high on the first of July, Canada's national birthday.

A radio announcer was describing the big holiday, or "hauliday," as he said, for I was back in English Canada. More than 16 million Canadians speak English, and nearly half of them live in Ontario. Their language has a unique flavor— spelled flavour, if you please. Every phrase becomes a question, often sprinkled with *eh?* It's a polite, tentative habit that constantly asks, "Do you follow me, am I clear?"

Canadian public servants often speak a rougher lingo. As I drove to Canada's capital of Ottawa, the newscast was playing a recent tape of "question period," a daily rite in Parliament. The questions were mainly critical speeches directed at the government; most replies brought Opposition groans and hisses. Democracy was alive and kicking, but mainly at partisan footballs. I hoped to hear more civil talk on Canada Day, the anniversary of Confederation.

Ottawa lies on the Ottawa River, dividing Quebec and Ontario. Queen Victoria chose this capital site and commissioned the lofty Gothic spires that crown Parliament Hill. Canadians at first called the town "Westminster in the Wilderness," and Ottawa still preserves a strong Anglo feel. Today the patriotic speeches were bilingual—but Canadian troops paraded by in the uniform of British Empire, Victorian red jackets and tall black bearskins. Ordinary citizens wore maple-leaf flags, stuck in a lapel or hatband, flying from bikes and baby carriages.

On this family holiday, George Mobley and I walked with Kathy Dobbin and her youngsters, Sarah and Michael, in a circuit of open-air events. A public relations manager for the national capital, Kathy came well supplied: maps, a picnic lunch, "also sun lotion, if we need it." The day was fair and hot, so many strollers wore brief attire—shorts, tank tops, an occasional string bikini. Along Wellington Street all offices were closed, except for the Bank of Canada. "Wall Street is working today," Kathy noted; "maybe our bankers rest on July 4!"

Canada Day celebrates not independence but a cautious alliance of French and English Canada. On Victoria Island we saw performers who represented the nation, with touches of provincial pride. Quebec sent jugglers and acrobats, masters of aerial balance; Newfoundland offered a fiddle band. After some toe-tapper jigs they closed with the stately national song, "O Canada." Crossing the river to Hull, Quebec, we piled on a free shuttle bus. "Our museums and outdoor concerts are also free," said Kathy. "We're known as the free-for-all capital."

On the waterfront at Jacques Cartier Park some sailboards were moving sleepily in the warm, light breezes. Down the river came swifter transport, a 36-foot freight canoe paddled by stout voyageurs. Dressed in buckskin jackets and rainbow sashes, they came ashore to the crowd's admiring applause. One of the crew was Ken Roberts, a canoe historian: "Imagine this boat coming out of the mist, loaded with fur and bound for Montreal. Out in the lake-and-woods country, a man could travel 50 miles a day; up to 7,000 miles a season. The voyageurs went everywhere, and a million Brits followed them."

The mood in Hull was quietly festive; back in Ottawa some Brits were getting rowdy. Young folks crowded into the outdoor beer gardens, carousing noisily; elders sipped at pints and mourned the country's future. But as night fell everyone stood and cheered the evening finale, a grand fireworks display in the sky above

More than single strand, the Trans-Canada braids and splits as it crosses the nation's most populous, wealthiest, and most industrialized province. Georgian Bay and Lake Superior dominate the highway's southern route. Northward stretch woodlands splashed by myriad waterways, merging with swampy muskeg in western Ontario.

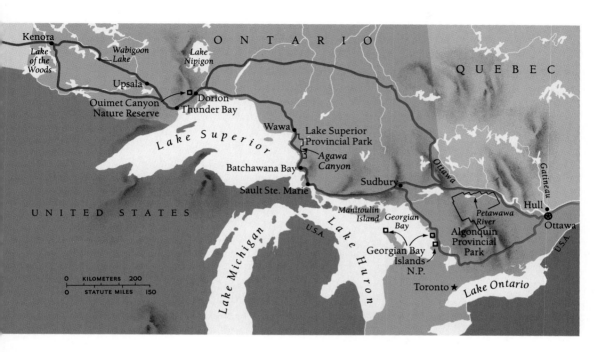

Parliament Hill. I walked home through streets littered with debris, yet at dawn they were swept and washed clean. A workman smiled at my surprise: "The beer cans? A boy and his sister got 'em for scrap. We take a bit of pride, eh?"

That morning George and I drove a few miles north of Ottawa to meet Bill Mason, who lives on a lake in the Gatineau Hills. His driveway sign is a canoe paddle, its handle curving into a hockey blade. Eight canoes lay near the house; two cars wore racks for hauling boats. The Masons may be Canada's best-known canoeists, for Bill has featured his family in several canoeing books and films, the latter shot for Canada's National Film Board. "I've returned to my first love now, painting," he said. "Nobody looks at a picture and says 'What's the plot?'"

On the top floor of their log home, the Masons have built a studio-production center. Bill and his wife, Joyce, share one wall—his drawing board and her computer. "Paul's Corner" is for their son, a rising cartoonist. Paul and his sister, Becky, both art school graduates, also work as canoe guides. Becky paints in a separate studio, just down the road: "We have completely different styles," Bill explained, "and neither of us takes advice." But they all love to canoe, so we spread out maps and began to plan a journey.

Ontario resembles a giant leaping fish, its back and belly arched between Hudson Bay and the Great Lakes. The shape is appropriate, since Ontario shimmers with lakes and rivers, and offers some of Canada's best sportfishing. The province is immense, a half-million square miles, second to Quebec's area but about one-third more populous. One of every three Canadians lives in Ontario—and most cling to the fishtail, between Michigan and New York. There lie Canada's big cities and factories, pumping out 40 percent of the national income; but Bill was looking north.

He traced several streams that course down

into the blue expanses of Superior, Huron, and Georgian Bay: "Canoes are made for that country. They're agile in rapids, light to carry but strong enough to cross the big lakes. I love that wild shore of Superior. On a foggy day it's like paddling on the inside of a milk jug." For our journey we chose the Petawawa River, a family favorite: "Good rapids and campsites," Bill said, "and the shores are lined with big sugar-loaf hills." Days later George and I drove 150 miles west with the Masons. At Lake Traverse, our four canoes headed into the watery maze of Algonquin Provincial Park.

Algonquin Park has more than 1,500 lakes, Ontario more than a quarter-million. Their combined surface area would cover Washington State, if the water ever slowed down. Bill shaped a broad dome with his hands: "The water is fast here because all these lakes and rivers drain quickly off the Shield." Spread across most of eastern Canada, the Canadian Shield is North America's ancient stone core. Its Precambrian rock has endured for three-quarters of the earth's existence. Eons of rain, snow, and moving ice have exposed the Shield, a stable mass but not as resistant as its name implies. When rock meets water, the water always wins.

At Big Thompson Rapids, I stood and watched the smooth dark current suddenly slip and spill downward, torn into tumbling white confusion. Bill and Paul studied the waves that curled back upstream, signs of hidden boulders. A "roller" wave could roll the boats; a "keeper" would grab and hold whatever entered its clutches. "You never get blasé about these rivers," Bill said. "With water levels constantly changing, they're different on every run."

Bill showed me how to read the river: A V-pattern on the surface pointing downstream indicates safe passage; one pointing upstream

means a rock. Just beyond such rocks lie eddies, brief havens of calm water. We portaged all of our gear, then watched Bill, Paul, and Becky shoot down Big Thompson Rapids. They made their solo runs look easy, like paddling down a staircase: some eggbeater swirls to the rear, a hard dig on the left, and they floated together in an eddy.

That night we camped on a river island, just a half-acre rocky knoll that soon felt like home. In the few minutes that I took to erect a tent, the Masons raised two canvas lean-tos, gathered and chopped wood, started a fire and boiled tea. On the cook table, an upended canoe, they arranged a kitchen. Out of canvas packs came utensils, food, spices, and snacks for the hungry—everyone qualified. Bill handled the packs with affection: "I've had some of these for 35 years. Before this trip I oiled the straps, got the rivets and seams back in shape. They're patched and re-patched, but still going."

So is Bill, after a lifetime spent in wilderness travel. Over dinner he talked about his early years: "As a young fellow I worked in ad agencies to support my canoeing. Every year I'd break the summer out, quit my job and go to the lakes. I guided canoe trips, was a camp counselor, but mostly I roamed. My food? Oh, pemmican made from ground beef and dried fruit, dried peas and carrots—hard as rocks—and whatever fish I caught. I'd go for five months, from break-up to freeze-up, and then find a winter job. My employers thought I was the original hippie."

After marriage—and a canoeing honeymoon—Bill began to shoot wilderness films about lakes and rivers, bowhead whales and timber wolves. His family often worked as cast and crew: "You'd hardly call it work; more like adventure." At home in winter they played hockey and broom ball, a sort of ice-polo on foot. "A full-contact sport," Paul said, "until we passed a hundred pounds. When we were smaller, we bounced better." Becky skated for a hockey team

SARAH LEEN (ABOVE); MAGGIE STEBER (OPPOSITE)

Lock gates close behind cabin cruisers and a
voyageur canoe entering the Rideau Canal from
the Ottawa River. Built for battles that never blazed,
the canal runs 123 miles from Ottawa to the Lake
Ontario port of Kingston. Fear of American attacks
following the War of 1812 prompted the canal's
design in 1826 as an alternative to the exposed St.
Lawrence. Today, its scenic route through 49 locks,
two rivers, and untold lakes draws boaters such as
Guy and Lise LaFontaine of Montreal (above).

at school: "The boys couldn't get the puck past me. They got very upset." Bill and Paul's new passion is telemark skiing. "It's the same thrill as rapids," said Paul: "making fast turns and trying to stay alive. . . ." Joyce interrupted: "Speak for yourself. I'm the only sane person in this family."

The next day I paddled with Becky, who coached me through strokes for running rapids. Soon I was steering us through rock gardens, patches of exposed boulders. For a 23-year-old, she had plenty of experience: "I think the folks brought me home from the hospital in a canoe."

We camped that evening by a set of ominous rapids, Crooked Chute. Here the river made several sharp, twisting turns while passing down a long trough between house-size boulders. Bill had seen many bad accidents here, including one death a few years ago. "People just won't recognize how dangerous rapids can be. I didn't until I smashed a canoe to bits out in the bush and had to walk home."

We suffered no mishaps at Crooked Chute, again portaging the gear while Bill, Paul, and Becky safely ferried our canoes. Tamer rapids provided an occasional bump on hidden rocks, for the Petawawa was running low. "No touches!" became our watchword, but by day's end the canoe bottoms were scraped and gouged aplenty. Yet spirits rode high, for this campsite lay near the Natch Rapids, below a sheer 200-foot cliff of pink-tinted Shield. We stayed there two days, an interlude spent in lazy pursuits—eating, sleeping, debating the next meal's menu. For exercise, hikers climbed the cliff or gathered firewood. At sundown, Paul and Becky paddled through a canoe ballet, boats leaning in long, slow arcs on the glassy water.

We hear that family life is waning these days, but the Masons have not joined that trend. Throughout the trip I saw them laugh and work together, lots of teasing and jokes yet somehow never a fight. In taking my leave, I complimented Joyce on this harmony: "It's odd, because we're

all so strong-minded. That's the way Bill and I were at the start. My parents thought he was a bum. We got engaged, he went off for a year, and my friends gave it no chance. But I stayed in love with him, because he was such a terrific guy."

My wife also lives with a wanderer, but sometimes we can journey together. After all my solo miles across Canada, Bonnie joined me in Ottawa to help with the Ontario driving. An English teacher on vacation, she brought along a bag of books to read—schoolwork, I thought, till I noticed an Agatha Christie. We bade farewell to George, who was going east, and turned west on the Trans-Canada.

Beyond Ottawa the highway splits into north and south sections; we chose the latter. The season was now high summer, and along the unmowed roadside we spied daylilies, black-eyed Susans, grasses with fat red seed heads, cool banks of green fern. But always in Ontario, water dominates. In a few hours we reached the broad blue expanse of Georgian Bay.

Often called "the sixth Great Lake," Georgian Bay is a Connecticut-size arm of Lake Huron, dotted with 30,000 islands. Glacial action formed all the Great Lakes, as ice spread south and gouged out basins, then filled them with meltwater when the glaciers retreated northward. Together these lakes comprise the world's largest body of fresh water, an undulant sea in the North American heartland. At Honey Harbour we boarded a shuttle boat bound for Beausoleil Island, the largest of 77 isles in Georgian Bay Islands National Park. Our skipper, Eric Bennett, threaded his boat around tiny cottage crags, summer homes perched on a few yards of land. The day was bright and hot. Fishing boats trolled by; sunbathers sprawled on docks like so many basking turtles.

On Beausoleil we found beautiful sun, plus

trails that encircle the island and its shoreline campsites. We chose the Christian Path, which runs past an old cemetery; deep in the woods we had to outrun pagan swarms of mosquitoes. Back on the shuttle, copilot Tracy Nicholson noted our bites: "The bugs come out only a few weeks a year. That seems to make them meaner."

Tracy grew up in Honey Harbour, one of a dozen children: "Six boys and six girls, all of us taught by Mother—she practically ran the grade school." In fall Tracy would enter grade 13, an extra year of training offered by Ontario high schools: "I'll take three courses in math before university study." On our return trip, she took the wheel and safely triangulated us to shore.

Beyond Georgian Bay the Trans-Canada enters a sparsely populated region that contains a wealth of raw materials. Besides water and timber, the Shield provides such vital minerals as copper, iron, and—in the area near Sudbury—the world's largest supply of nickel. Mining has drawn inhabitants here since prehistoric times. On Manitoulin Island archaeologists have found quartz blades and scrapers at a 9,000-year-old Indian quarry. To the Ojibwa, Manitoulin meant home of Gitchi Manitou, the Great Spirit. Some strong force does seem to govern this island. Waiting for a swing bridge to close, I turned on a portable CB radio—and overheard a conversation in North Carolina, 800 miles distant.

On the road, license plates zipped by us from Texas, Kentucky, Connecticut, while just offshore, barges filled with grain and coal chugged down the St. Lawrence Seaway. This system of natural waterways, locks, and channels gives Canada and the States a 2,300-mile trade route to the Atlantic. The seaway can admit the majority of the world's saltwater vessels, lifting them up and down the 560-foot drop between here and Montreal. Those long, slow barges provide cheap transport of mid-continent goods, an important factor in meeting foreign competition. For every Ford or Chevy that passed us, a Toyota or Honda soon followed.

At Sault Ste. Marie, home of the "Soo" Locks between Huron and Superior, we parked the van and boarded the Algoma Central Railway for a brief northern excursion. The day was just right for not driving: cool and gusty, with intermittent showers. Rain pattered on windows as passengers settled into the comforts of a low-speed train, 40 miles per hour. Children roamed the aisles or peeked at neighbors; fragrances of hotcakes and coffee wafted in from the dining car. I lost some appetite as the train swayed on a long curving trestle over a sheer hundred-foot pitch down into rushing waters.

Our route led into the heart of Algoma, a wilderness district lying east of Lake Superior. Once mainly a freight line to haul ore and timber, this railway now carries more than a hundred thousand passengers a year. Some are hunters, who will journey north to the moose swamps in the James Bay region; others are modern voyageurs. Canoeists buy a ticket to remote stops, disembark there and head west along white-water streams. Most of the riders are daytrippers, drawn to the ease of taking an armchair journey through Algoma scenery—made famous after World War I by the Group of Seven, Canada's first modern landscape painters.

On this dark, wet day, the country became its own canvas. Heads swiveled as the train passed from walls of black spruce, streaked with white birch, to ponds edged by meadows of rainbent grass. Loons drifted in pairs on leaden bays; lakeside cabins appeared, smoke lifting from the chimneys. We serpentined up through hills near 2,200-foot Ogidaki Mountain, then descended into a narrow river gap, Agawa Canyon. During a two-hour layover here, most passengers stayed on board. We followed a handful of explorers up 372 slippery wooden stairsteps to look out over the canyon. Kevin and Pat Cassidy, a couple in yellow slickers, eyed the swollen Agawa River. "A nice canoe ride," Kevin began. "But on the train," said Pat, "we'll sleep our way home."

Next morning Bonnie and I left Sault Ste. Marie and drove north. The road cut across highlands to Batchawana Bay and our first glimpse of Lake Superior, largest and deepest of the Great Lakes. Of equal interest to me was a roadside marker near Chippewa Falls: "This plaque stands approximately at the halfway point of the Trans-Canada Highway, which runs from St. John's, Newfoundland, to Victoria, British Columbia." I stood at Mile 2,430, near the center of my journey, beside a stream flowing into wide blue waters. I was at midsummer in Ontario, halfway across the nation. An hour back we had passed a patriotic billboard—for me, an itinerary: "One Canada, from Sea to Sea."

As we skirted the shoreline of Superior, I kept one eye on Bonnie, who is a compulsive rock hound. Addicted to the heft and grain of beach stones, she smuggles sacks home from journeys, against her family's counsel. The Precambrian rocks along this shore made piles of tempting rubble: They broke the surface in jagged heaps of deep ruby or pale chalk, shining with the iridescent hues of green, black, and gold. Road-cuts exposed more wonders, 80-foot pillars with a glinting mica sheen. The Rock Shop appeared: Just one quick stop? Its owner was stony-faced, but honest. I asked Ken Edwards if he located here for the area's choice rocks. "Nope," he said: "It has a lot of tourists."

In late afternoon we entered Lake Superior Provincial Park, nearly 600 square miles of hills and shores by "the shining Big-Sea-Water" of Longfellow's epic, *The Song of Hiawatha*. No single American poem is better known or less read than *Hiawatha*, a classic example of Indian lore—as told by whites. Based on library research, not direct observation, the poem recounts Iroquois and *(Continued on page 100)*

Rafters toss a legs-up salute to the power of the Ottawa River at McCoy Chute. Largest tributary of the St. Lawrence, the Ottawa served as a route into the interior for explorers, fur traders, and missionaries. Today, abundant rapids and relatively warm waters make it a highly popular recreational river.

Savoring a life spent in the Canadian wilds, canoeist and filmmaker Bill Mason (left) tends a crackling streamside cook fire. Author Howarth and photographer Mobley joined Mason and his family for a week on the Petawawa River in 3,000-square-mile Algonquin Provincial Park, Ontario's oldest preserve. Mason's wife, Joyce (above, at right), takes her turn at cooking at their camp near Crooked Chute. Low water caused by exceptional midsummer heat plagued the trip, forcing numerous canoe draggings through normally brisk white-water runs such as Little Thompson Rapids (right).

FOLLOWING PAGES: Morning mists shroud Bill Mason as he solos below the Natch Rapids. He calls the Petawawa River "one of my favorite trips—a great variety of scenery, from lakes with high hills to narrow gorges and cliffs."

Ojibwa legends of a great brave who becomes the defender and tamer of his people. He teaches them to plant corn, build bark canoes, harvest the woods and waters—and to accept the coming palefaces, who bring a new religion. Hiawatha paddles away in the end; his people remain to face civilization.

We read the Indian past differently now, and one reason arose before me at Agawa Rock. In 1958 a scholar named Selwyn Dewdney paddled along this shore in search of pictographs. In the region he had found almost 300 rock art sites, remote places where Indians rested and prayed, drew spirit pictures to calm the big lake and bring forth its fish. Here, where a rock ledge slopes abruptly into water, Dewdney found a crevice containing a sacred image of a powerful spirit, the manitou Mishipizhiw: "a huge animal with crested back and horned head, there was no mistaking him . . . my fourteen months' search was over."

I ventured out on the wave-washed ledge to see this painting, drawn in a red ocher pigment made from crushed rock and fish oil: the horned beast, a man on a horse, six men in canoes. The meaning is unknown, its source perhaps a trance induced by fasting and prayer. To draw this manitou was to invoke the strongest deity, host of the water and father of all storms. Now rains and waves are slowly erasing the paint—helped by visitors who can't resist a touch. The Ojibwa fishing camps in this area are up to 2,000 years old; this painting, several hundred. By then the palefaces were coming, I thought, and looked up to see three inching toward me. They stood in silence, read the warning signs, and touched.

Back in the parking lot, Bonnie and I struck up some talk with two residents of Algoma, Corrine Thomas and Angèle Quesnel-Mawhinney. Both teach in a French grade school in Wawa, a few miles north, and they thought Ontario was the most genuinely bilingual province. "We don't fight over it here," Angèle said. "It's for the betterment of children to know two languages." She spoke French to her son, Marc, but at times marshaled him with English: "I mean it, get over here right now!" Corrine, an Acadian from New Brunswick, is now loyal to the northland: "I love having all this nature; it's like living for free in Tom Thomson's paintings."

As we drove at sunset toward Wawa, the evening light evoked memories of that artist. A brooding loner, Tom Thomson camped and sketched throughout Algonquin Park in the early 1900s. His stark, strongly colored images of jack pines and autumn shores inspired fellow artists, who followed him to the park. Thomson was pure Canadian, van Gogh with a backpack. One evening in July 1917, he paddled down Canoe Lake and was never again seen alive, the victim of either a drowning or a homicide. His artist friends later formed the Group of Seven and relocated to the Algoma District. Now the movement's legacy lay here, on the shoreline of Superior, where the falling sun flamed on striped Indian blanket rocks. As the water darkened, cars turned on their lights. They made bright, moving points against the big lake and sky, like facets on a gem.

The next morning was sharp and cool, but up the road we found evidence of a bigger chill. At a gas station in White River, the sign read: "Coldest Spot in Canada, -72 Degrees." I asked the clerk about this claim: "That was back in the 1930s," she said. "The Yukon holds the record now, and they can keep it, too." Ontario has also seen summer days of 110°F, but the real heat lies far below its surface. Over millions of years, a fiery magma rose to form the Shield, heating upper layers into new minerals, then cooling as solid crystals of granite, mica, quartz—and, in rare pockets, precious metals and gems. King Midas must have touched the north shore of

"Shining Big-Sea-Water," Longfellow dubbed Lake Superior in his 1855 epic, The Song of Hiawatha. *Inspiring vistas and thick pine forests still mark much of its shoreline, as in this view of Agawa Bay in Lake Superior Provincial Park. Long a seasonal gathering place for Ojibwa Indians, Agawa Bay harbors pictographs of the manitou Mishipizhiw, legendary cause of Superior's notorious storms.*

Superior: It has North America's richest gold mine at Hemlo, and—near Thunder Bay—a half-dozen of the world's best amethyst mines.

Near Dorion we turned onto a dirt road and proceeded to the Ontario Gem Mining Company. Signboards touted the virtues of amethyst: It brings good luck, raises intelligence, wards off disease and drunkenness. Credit cards are accepted, and "All Rock Must Be Paid For." Although considered a gemstone, amethyst is inexpensive at the source. Inside the shop, co-owner Pat Marino offered us a choice: "You can buy cleaned and cut stones here, or mine your own out back," she said.

With goggles, a hammer, and bucket, we strolled through the woods to a hillside, partly exposed by bulldozer. From the rubble rose lavender blooms: clover, healwort, wandering vetch; common flowers growing amid the rock's jeweled glints. When we saw amethyst crystals, winking purple sparks in the sun, even I caught rock-hound fever.

Noting this interest, Pat and her husband, Peter, invited us to visit a new vein "and see our big discovery." On a hillside Peter dropped a stone down a dark cavity: silence, then a distant splash. "It's a vug, or gas pocket, which runs along a fault. One blast and the top popped off

like a manhole cover. You should see the crystals inside." So I dropped into rough, damp blackness, but my flashlight caught thousands of crystal points, exactly six-sided and clustered in rich accretions of red, violet, or rusty plum. A brown oxide scale covered many: "We soak them," Pat said, "then lots of scrubbing with detergent. Not too great for the hands."

Peter likes this low-tech form of mining. "It's quiet; even blasting is just a little thump or puff you feel in the chest. Mostly I work with a crowbar and hammer." He rapped on top of some quartz veins, listening for a hollow tock, tock. "If it's hollow, the crystals are below."

Back at the processing sheds, we examined tables of amethyst sorted by size and color. "Another discovery is in shaping gems," said Pat, who has grown expert at designing jewelry. "We smooth them in tumbler machines, ship them to Germany for cutting and faceting, then work them into every possible setting."

The Marinos have run this family business for ten years, chopping it out of the bush like pioneers. A Minnesotan, Pat has had to make her way among Canadians. "Americans sometimes get branded as pushy because they go for what they want. Living here can be like walking through a maze." Native to Ontario, Peter did not disagree: "But still, where else could I work in an environment like this, going at my own pace? Every day I'm looking for treasure, and the big reward is finding something unexpected."

Laden with rocks, we returned to the road, its northern and southern sections once again merged into a single Trans-Canada—now with an added label, "Terry Fox Courage Highway." On a bluff overlooking Lake Superior and the city of Thunder Bay, many cars had stopped to pay respects at a monument to Terrance Stanley Fox, who may be Canada's first truly national hero. Born in British Columbia in 1958, Terry Fox was a fleet long-distance runner when he lost his right leg to cancer at the age of 18. A man of remarkable courage and idealism, he planned a "Marathon of Hope" across Canada to raise funds for cancer research. Running mostly on the Trans-Canada, he began in April 1980 at St. John's, Newfoundland, and averaged a marathon each day, about 26 miles.

The sight of his strong young body, striding on a skeletal man-made limb, stirred Canadians into a rare display of national unity. Donations flooded in as Fox ran across the country, speaking with fervent hope about his dreams of defeating cancer, ". . . because somewhere the hurting must stop." After he had run more than 3,300 miles and raised 24 million dollars, his own cancer returned, forcing him to end his effort seven miles west of this spot. His monument, a bronze statue atop Ontario granite, is a runner forever striding on, face lifted to his western goal. In recalling Terry Fox, Peter Marino spoke for many: "Canada opened to him; what a big hero he was."

We pulled into Thunder Bay, largest port on Lake Superior, and drove by a shore dominated by the trappings of modern transportation. Here the eastern waterways meet the western rail system; hundreds of boxcars were dumping prairie wheat into the world's largest grain elevators, millions of bushels waiting for shipment down the St. Lawrence Seaway.

Two centuries ago the bustling trade here was in furs, brought by canoes nearly 1,500 miles from the far Northwest. The canoes arrived at Fort William, today a reconstructed log village where a costumed staff enacts historical roles. In a room piled with smooth beaver pelts, Alistair Gordon explained how they became fashionable top hats in London. A T-shirted visitor looked dubious: "Why, lad," Alistair said, "I'd be in trouble if caught without the right top hat."

West of Thunder Bay, builders of the Trans-Canada faced one of their most difficult tasks:

Visitors gaze from an overlook into Ontario's "grandest canyon"—the main attraction of Ouimet Canyon Nature Reserve, some 50 miles northeast of Lake Superior's Thunder Bay. Born of ancient igneous rock later sculptured by glacial action, the steep, fluted cliffs keep the riverless gorge largely in shadow—enabling it to shelter arctic flora usually restricted to colder latitudes.

crossing the lake-and-muskeg country that rolls some 300 miles to Manitoba. Muskeg refers to the region's wet, spongy forest of spruce and tamarack, a forbidding swampland laced with rocky outcrops. The highway leaps the water on long causeways, threading its way around lakes so plentiful they seem flung from an outstretched hand.

Towns are small and widely separated, mainly devoted to forestry. Sawmills and pulp mills went by, each with its distinct odor. Past Wabigoon Lake we encountered more than 280,000 acres of forest that burned in 1980 after a lightning strike. The trees still stood, ranks of gray quills bristling from pink granite ridges. A desolate scene, this forest gone to fire before its prime, yet the flames that seared the old trees also sowed many new ones, popping open the cones of jack pines and spreading their seeds.

We passed on, threading our way along Lake of the Woods, a huge domain—nearly 60,000 miles of shoreline, dotted with more than 14,000 islands. In other seasons here the Indians harvest wild rice and trappers prey on beaver and marten. To the north lay a vast lake-and-forest wilderness, familiar to me from many summers spent in a family cabin near Sioux Lookout. No time now to go there for bass and muskie, to lie on sunstruck rocks or hear at night the cool, silvery laughter of loons. Ahead the road ran west, beyond Ontario's shining waters and into the grasslands of the Prairie Provinces.

*As reveling voyageurs once danced, so now do children romp to the same tunes
outside Old Fort William, a ten-acre reconstruction of the fur-trading town begun
in 1803 by the North West Company, Canada's first transcontinental concern.*

*FOLLOWING PAGES: Tiny Catholic Church of Upsala, some 90 miles northwest of
Thunder Bay, stands awash in a daisy sea in sparsely populated western Ontario.*

Ranks of sunflowers turn faces to the west on a farm near Carberry, Manitoba, easternmost of the Prairie Provinces. Grown primarily for oil, sunflowers supplement traditional grain crops such as wheat, barley, oats, and rye. On Canada's fertile plains, occasional ranches and towns interrupt immense cultivated tracts—where stretches of virgin grasslands once rolled to the Rockies.

ACROSS

THE GRASSLANDS

Prairie Provinces

In Manitoba the land soon changed from wet forest to rolling prairie, open to the sun and wind that blew across a wide green horizon. The van settled into miles of fast travel, rolling down a straight four-lane highway toward the west. I was now driving the stretch of the Trans-Canada that engineers had built swiftly, across the plains of southern Manitoba, Saskatchewan, and Alberta. The road spans a wide belt of grasslands, farm and ranch country that rises in a long smooth incline toward the Canadian Rockies. Soon I passed a sign marking 96° west, the longitudinal center of Canada.

I was tempted to compare this land to Kansas and Nebraska, but the Prairie Provinces have their own character. Forming one-fifth of the Canadian landmass, they contained vast Ice Age lakes whose sediments built a fertile southern crescent. Eighty percent of Canada's field crops grow there, on such wide tracts that the country seems one continuous farm. The colors and squared angles of fields make a vast geometry, mosaics built from living tile. Equally varied are the region's people, European immigrants who retained their customs on this new frontier.

Bonnie and I glimpsed that tradition at Steinbach, where a tall Dutch-style windmill marks the Mennonite Heritage Village. A long history of religious persecution and forced migration brought these Dutch-German Anabaptists to Manitoba in 1874. Hardworking farmers, they banded together in compact villages for solidarity and shared labor. At first they lived in sod huts—"Rained outside for one day, inside for two," explained a guide. Later they built house-barns, just a short hallway separating stable from kitchen. Today the village restaurant still serves borscht, fried sausage, and *vareniki*—stuffed noodles. The cooks gossip in a soft, breathy Low German, their mother tongue.

From Steinbach we drove 30 miles west to Winnipeg, home of 600,000—fully half the population of Manitoba. Downtown Winnipeg is an urban cluster of banks and warehouses, crossed by east-west tracks of the Canadian Pacific Railway. Headquarters of the nation's grain market, Winnipeg is an affluent, bustling city with symphony and ballet, also enough ethnic dining to stuff a gourmand silly—Korean, Yugoslavian, Polynesian, even Chilean in this far northern clime. The city is a tapestry of folk cultures, celebrated in a round of seasonal festivals and daily worship at local churches. On a drive we passed several buildings topped with onion domes, Ukrainian Orthodox and Catholic cathedrals.

"I have a beautiful memory from childhood of Easter Sunday, when we brought the *pysanka* to church." Ted Wasylyshen smiled and lifted an egg, inscribed with bright swirls of color. "Pysanka means egg-writing; you make designs with a pen and hot wax, then dip the egg in dyes. At Easter we gave eggs to friends and children, and that gave everyone a new lease on life." In their Winnipeg home, Ted and his wife, Eve, maintain a large private collection of Ukrainian Easter eggs. "No two designs are ever exactly alike," Eve said as she inscribed a fine continuous circle. "The egg itself represents new life. My favorite design? The wheat. I love the head of wheat."

The ancestral crop in Manitoba was a grand expanse of tall, waving grass, often the height of a man. Early French explorers called this treeless country *prairie,* their word for meadow, and they marveled at its lush abundance of wild fruit and game. Today one of the few remnant patches of tallgrass prairie stands in suburban Winnipeg, surrounded by tract houses. The Living Prairie Museum is a former dairy pasture, 40 acres no one ever plowed. Beside clumps of waist-high grass Bonnie found scattered pink roses and bergamot, purple thistles and creamy milkweed— just a few of the more than 160 kinds of plants that thrive here. Despite this profusion, the native prairie plants are facing competition.

To naturalist Cheryl Shea, certain species spell the trouble: "We have some recent invaders

From Ontario the Trans-Canada Highway sweeps some 1,000 miles west across southern Manitoba, Saskatchewan, and Alberta—Canada's agricultural heartland. Eighty percent of the nation's field crops derive from these billowing prairies, which a century ago promised freedom and prosperity to eastern European immigrants. Their descendants here still cling proudly to cherished Old World customs.

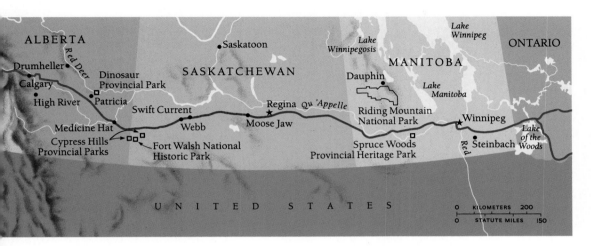

here," she said, pointing to encroaching stands of wolf willow and aspen. "Most shrubs and trees couldn't survive on the native prairie. Wildfires and herds of bison kept it clear." Now the museum staff must set controlled fires to prevent invaders from shading out the native plants. "Big bluestem, the tallest grass, is getting sparse," Cheryl noted, "and sweet clover is starting to arrive." Other plants are also upstarts—such as the misnamed Canada thistle. "You know, Americans were the ones who called it that, but the weed actually came from Eurasia."

Like the plants, human migrants invaded the grasslands and began to reshape its face. Early Indian hunters left traces of tent circles and fire rings; fur traders built walled outposts, such as Lower Fort Garry just north of Winnipeg. Along the Red River, farmers planted wheat in long, narrow lots—the system for sharing waterfront I had seen along the St. Lawrence. Then Canada, about to acquire the Red River Valley, began to map it in square-mile townships, the English method of land survey. Those lines of force clashed in the North-West Rebellion of 1885, Canada's last civil war.

At the doorway of a small clapboard cottage in south Winnipeg, René Vielfaure scanned a nearby field. "That was the family farm of Louis Riel; four lots wide and two miles long. He was raised at the other end, and it was here that his body lay in state." René tends Riel House, a memorial to the prairie people called Métis, or mixed bloods. Descendants of Indian women and French trappers, the Métis feared Canada's westward expansion.

Riel rallied his people with fiery speeches, René told me, securing their land and language rights prior to the creation of Manitoba in 1870. But elements hostile to his cause later forced Riel into exile. He returned to Canada in 1884 and led a series of skirmishes; in 1885 he was caught and hanged for treason. The North-West Rebellion died with him. Outside Riel House, René saw goldfinches fluttering over thistles. "It's sad to see this land go back to weeds."

From Winnipeg I drove west alone, for Bonnie had flown home with plans to rejoin me at Calgary. Now the Trans-Canada ran past miles of tall sunflower fields, guarded by clacking blackbirds. This soil was sloping and sandy, the upper beach of a vanished glacial lake. At Carberry I turned south to visit the Spirit Sands, exposed dunes in Spruce Woods Provincial Heritage Park. Trudging *(Continued on page 116)*

Spirited Cossack dance troupe performs during Dauphin's annual Ukrainian folk festival. Parades and native foods and crafts mark the Manitoba celebration, an opportunity for the 500,000 or so Canadians claiming Ukrainian descent to foster ties. A young Ukrainian (above) wears jewelry and an intricately embroidered blouse typical of her ancestral home.

FOLLOWING PAGES: ". . . a light to set a painter wild, a light pure, glareless, and transparent." So writer Wallace Stegner described the dome of sky above his beloved Canadian prairie. Stegner's pure light washes over an abandoned Manitoba homestead standing in a field of rapeseed, also called canola—a crop prized for the oil it yields.

through ten square miles of wind-drifted sand, I could see why Indians once called this a spirit place. A hot, dry breeze whispered along the dune tops, sifting golden sand into my foot tracks. Before me, a hognose snake twisted away, and in time the dunes also move, gathering and spilling forward in rippled waves. But wind-blown seeds move faster; soon grass and trees may blanket this region. Over the past 9,000 years, the Spirit Sands have shrunk from 2,500 square miles down to these remaining ten.

Going 75 miles northwest, I passed from desert to Riding Mountain National Park, a 1,200-square-mile ecosystem of such diversity that it was honored as a UNESCO Biosphere Reserve in 1986. Dan Weedon calls the area "the natural playground of Manitoba—lakes, cottages, camping, and some of the best wildlife anywhere." A former park naturalist, Dan now guides nature tours across this high plateau: "There's no major peak here, just a long ridge that rises 1,500 feet above the prairie. It's an island where grasslands meet forest, a crossroads for a great variety of birds and mammals."

To prove his point Dan drove me past Wasagaming, a resort village with ice cream parlors and lawn bowlers, to a nearby marsh. Deep in the lily pads a giant bull moose was feeding. After a languid dip underwater, he emerged with hunks of dripping green browse. "Just a mouthful for him," Dan said. "Will you look at that six-foot rack? That's some sight for kids to see." Minutes later we paused at the park's eastern gate and looked out across miles of broad, flat plains. "Number one land in Canada," said Dan; "high-priced because it's good, rich soil with a long growing season."

Dan, who farms a bit himself, wants to see less land planted to crops and more habitat saved for wildlife. "Years ago, every puddle was a duck factory, but now the population has plummeted. We've got to stop draining marshes and burning the nesting cover; maybe stop hunting ducks for a while, too." Less farming might also reduce Canada's large grain surpluses, a chronic problem that lowers prices. "Some people say, 'You got to open land up,' even though they can't make money on what they've plowed. We need to let it rest, stop thinking of this as frontier country."

But Stan Andrechuk's memories of his boyhood 70 years ago are hard to forget: "I was raised on a homestead, a quarter section—160 acres. We lived in a log house with thatched roof and clay-plastered walls. Just had kerosene lights. My Dad used to work with oxen in the fields. He hired out as carpenter and shoemaker, too. That was hard country to make a living in, but if we had plenty milk and eggs, then we were never hungry. At Christmas we baked *kolach;* at Easter the *paska* and gifts of pysanka." He saw me nod. "So, you understand Ukrainian?" No, but I had met some egg-artists in Winnipeg. "Ah, sure, but we do it best in Dauphin."

I had driven 30 miles north to this town of 10.000, most of them descended from Ukrainian immigrants. Of the half-million Ukrainians in Canada, two-thirds live in the three Prairie Provinces. Coming from one of Europe's renowned agricultural regions, they naturally migrated in the 1890s to western Canada, spurred by the promise of cheap land—and a free country. Stan and his wife, Minnie, visited the Soviet Ukraine last year: "Oh beautiful, but we don't want to live there. Always they told us what to do. Here, I'm glad to pay taxes—at least I got the income!"

After a coffee break at Sticky's—a diner crowded with men in overalls and feed caps—we stopped in the Ukrainian Festival office. Phones were ringing, for in late July the festival would draw 50,000 visitors to Dauphin for a four-day celebration of Ukrainian culture—food, dance, history, song. Helen Lazaruk Henderson was rehearsing the festival choir: "We have 38 voices, men and women singing in four-part harmony a cappella. This year we act out a whole wedding, with folk songs and dialogue." Mike Dudar planned to wear his traditional white shirt and red sash at all functions: "My favorite show is the Cossack men; last year—talk about dancing!—they made the crowd howl."

These elders spoke both Ukrainian and English, but they worried about the next generation. "Young people are not fluent in Ukrainian any more," Mike said. "We started this festival in 1966 because the old traditions were dying out." During those years Jan Kuzuchar tried living in Ontario, but now she's glad to be home: "I missed the Christmas and Easter customs, especially; they mean so much in family life." I was sorry to miss the festival, but it was time to go. Stan wished me well: "Come back on a holiday. Ukrainians like to have lots of holidays."

Now I pointed the van toward Saskatchewan, rolling across a plain that rose a foot per mile. Far ahead of me on the road lay heat mirages, bright mirrors that reflected distant trees. A hot July sun beat down through the windshield; bugs rattled off the hood into oblivion. The car radio played a doleful country tune, "Drop kick me, Jesus, through the goalposts of life. . . ." I turned it off and let the miles go by, passing villages with silver-domed churches and massive grain elevators, their broad walls and steep roofs rising like prairie cathedrals. In Yorkton, Saskatchewan, the local funeral parlor advised: "Drive Carefully. We'll Wait."

That evening I camped on the smooth green flanks of the "hidden" Qu'Appelle Valley, a broad water-cut depression in the prairie surface. Qu'Appelle means "who calls," the French rendering of an old Cree name. An Indian legend tells of spirits calling at night along the Qu'Appelle River, and perhaps some do still at the ancient burial mound above Crooked Lake. The river, so sluggish that it meanders in lazy curves across the valley's floodplain, forms a series of long shallow lakes, the summer home to waterfowl and campers.

After breaking camp the next morning, I paused at the valley rim to take in a long view of the Saskatchewan plains. In all directions the horizon made a thin dark edge to the wide bowl of sky. I imagined coming back here at harvest, when this country turns a deep burnt brown and geese fly south in high V-lines across a ruddy sun. In today's heat the main creatures about were ground squirrels, feeding on the roadside grasses. They sat erect to watch the van go by, then scattered when I honked.

A few miles down the Trans-Canada I met two more spectators, Clifford and Hazel Carson from San Diego. Hazel was photographing the flax and rapeseed fields, now in full color as a mass of swaying blue and yellow flowers. "Isn't it grand?" she exclaimed. "These fields put us in mind of home." Clifford grew up in southeastern Kansas, where he remembers growing flax. "We boiled it for home remedies, and used the liquid to flush out eyes or as a poultice to draw off poison. Sometimes for bellyaches we ate the stuff—it had long, messy strings." Today flax and rapeseed are pressed for their oil; the crops bring higher prices than wheat and help to diversify farm production.

As a boy, Clifford knew farming on a humble scale: "We didn't do nothing but try to raise a living; just feed ourselves and pay the bills. Nowadays people would rather work for eight hours and then do what they want." In fact, the Carsons were doing just that. "Since retirement we spend four to six months a year on the road in our camper," Hazel said. "This trip, we're going east to the Gaspé Peninsula." They would work their way home by October, after journeying nearly 10,000 miles. "My Dad never left Labette County," Clifford remarked. "Said he wouldn't go any farther than he could holler back." After they left, I moved out (Continued on page 122)

Financial adviser in the Baildon Hutterite Colony near Moose Jaw, Saskatchewan, John Hofer (right) sets aside duties to hold grandson Michael, one of 34 grandchildren. Weekly rotation of chores finds Lydia, left, and Annie Waldner baking bread in the colony's communal bakery. Though they embrace modern technology, the 70 members of the Anabaptist sect prefer plain dress; women wear polka-dot scarves, men black hats. Youngster Jonathan Wipf (left) sports a homemade cap.

FOLLOWING PAGES: Cathedrals of the prairie, grain elevators tower alongside railroad tracks on the Saskatchewan flatlands. Grain from here travels west to Vancouver or east to Thunder Bay, some destined for shipment worldwide.

into the field. The crops parted and closed about me, like waist-high water, and breezes stirred the stalks with a soft rustling clash. The field sounded alive, a great creature breathing in its lair. A meadowlark landed on a nearby fence post, preened and launched one full-throated song, straight to the sun. I could barely see its bright yellow breast against the blooming rapeseed, but nothing hid that high, sweet spray of sound.

For 20 miles the Trans-Canada ran due west toward the Saskatchewan capital of Regina. In early days Regina was called Pile O' Bones, after the heaps of bison remains found in slaughter traps set by Indians. The soil here is dense clay, dusty in dry seasons and a thick gumbo in wet. After a passing shower you can gain an extra three or four pounds just by walking around. But here rose Regina, queen of the prairie and home to 185,000. From ten miles out I could see the city springing up from the plains, a metropolis of skyscrapers on the board-flat earth.

Regina is also home to "Depot" Division, the training academy for Royal Canadian Mounted Police. No other country has an equivalent to the RCMP, Canada's defenders of law and order. Born in 1873 as the North-West Mounted Police, Mounties earned their fame with many legendary feats: hunting down criminals on horseback, making 150-mile dogsled patrols at 40 below zero. "Today we have members in every province," said Dave Pearce. "We travel in cars and snowmobiles, and our duties range from traffic control to fighting drugs and airline hijackers."

As training officer of "Depot" Division, Dave oversees the instruction of new recruits to the force. "We promise them a challenge, and they don't get cheated of it." The training program is paramilitary, rooted in Royal Irish Constabulary traditions of physical conditioning, weaponry, and parade drill. Out of this regimen comes not an army but a proud, strong corps of national police: "We have Indian constables on the reservations, bilingual constables in all provinces," Dave explained. "Of our 14,000 uniformed members strung across the country, all share the experience of training here."

Sgt. Claude Duret launched my daylong tour of the "Depot" grounds, a place members regard as their campus and boot camp. Troops of recruits were marching to classes; others doubletimed along the roads in cadenced unison. The latter groups all wore blue running shoes: "They run everywhere in the early weeks," Claude said, "until they've earned their marching orders." To reach graduation day each troop must become a crack parade unit, able to execute a 20-minute precision drill. In a beginning class, Cpl. Bob Gallup started the long process: "You DOZY men," he roared in full basso, "STAND to atTENtion!" Silence reigned as he walked the ranks, drill stick under one arm. "They're scared to death in these first classes," Claude murmured, "but in a few weeks confidence will take over."

In a nearby gym, recruits were hustling through calisthenic sets, shouting encouragement to team partners. One pair working at push-ups were Rosaire Bernard and Dennis Flint, at least twice the age of their troop-mates. I met those two as they put away a hasty lunch. Both had sought admission to the RCMP under relaxed age restrictions brought about by the recent Charter of Rights. Rosaire, a lean and muscled 47, was making history with an air of absolute conviction.

"I'm the oldest recruit ever, so the fellows call me Gramps. I'm holding up because I trained heavily last year after open heart surgery. After that I just had a sense that there was more in me to accomplish." Dennis had been a music teacher; at 39, his major goal was to become a policeman. "When I put on that scarlet tunic," he said, "half of my hometown will come to see me graduate."

Women compose about 7 percent of today's RCMP, and their ranks are steadily growing. Claude and I met Leanne Poch, a recruit on sick leave while recuperating from a leg injury. Determined to recover, she was dressed for an afternoon's long run. Claude offered her a marathoner's advice: "Start out slow, and don't push the pace till the last quarter." Outside, we found Superintendent Dave Pearce about to inspect the troop band, led by Constable Karen Pearce. "There's some history," said Claude. "We've never had a father and daughter in the same training division before."

After his last drill class for the day, Bob Gallup finished up my tour. His parade manner eased and gentled: "Let me show you some

nostalgia." We walked over to B Block and examined the stairwell floor, made of granite but in one spot worn an inch deep. "The troops come racing down these stairs for inspection, plant their left boots there and pivot out the door."

Departure is a constant theme at the Division. Troops come and go, graduating every few weeks, and the ceremony is unforgettable to those who trained together. "For six months they've lived and worked toward this goal, and the final drill is their last official act as a troop. I tell them, 'You may be a big macho Mountie, but when you hear that last command to dismiss, you're gonna break down.'" From here the members spread all over Canada, rarely to meet again. "If you run across a

troop-mate, it's like seeing a family member."

To the west of Regina I saw a wheeled irrigation line, the sign of approaching dry country. With its scant 15 inches of annual rainfall, this land still produces more than half of Canada's wheat. Once a glacial lake bed, the broad, flat Regina Plain now cloaks itself in spring wheat—turning a pale golden tan in late July, about a month before harvest. Even the highway median bears wheat, along with grain storage bins shaped like red coolie hats. The high plains have little strong relief, save for the dark forms of power poles and silos, beehive-shaped granaries and great pitched-roof elevators. I passed exits for Drinkwater, Moose Jaw, Eyebrow, Elbow, Friend, and Wartime. In flat country, naming towns must have been the local entertainment.

Beyond Swift Current the land began to lift into heaves and surges, wave-shaped moraines left by retreating glaciers. Once this region was all shortgrass prairie, good open range for bison and then cattle. Now fences edge the highway, and cows use underpasses made of culvert pipe. Most of the farms unfold in wide green and tan stripes, a dryland practice of planting and fallowing fields. Droughts here have killed off many dreams; abandoned homes and machinery still recall the dust-storm days of the 1930s. Many experts think plows should never have touched this range. Near Webb I walked in a field of ripe wheat. Every step filled the air with the buzz, whir, and drum of flying grasshoppers.

"Yes, the prairie is just about gone, and we might be soon." Jim Hartwick, naturalist at the Prairie Wildlife Interpretation Center, looked across its 1,100 acres of marsh and grassland to the drying bed of Goose Lake. After nesting all spring atop flax bales the geese had moved on, but these salty waters still attracted avocets and gulls to feed on brine shrimp. Those are natural changes in the prairie's cycle; the interpretation center was facing man-made woes. Cutbacks in federal funding may soon end interpretive services: "We get 10,000 visitors a year, but they won't stop to hike on trails if the staff's gone."

We walked up a long slope of grass, amid the warning calls of ground squirrels and birds. "The pipit hides well," Jim said, "yet in flight it sings constantly, a sort of musical rain." At the hilltop we surveyed broad rolling country, like a seabed waiting for water. Off in the distance, a tall thin dust devil spun across the fields. Below us spread a green, twisting channel lined with shrubs and berry bushes—a stream bed? "Coulee," said Jim, "from the French *couler, to flow.* They're like gutters, eroded by snow and rain. Good habitat for mice and deer." Two hawks soared above us, watching for signs of life scurrying down there.

Another 60 miles west, I turned off the Trans-Canada to detour through the Cypress Hills, provincial parks spanning Saskatchewan and Alberta. The roads became gravel and dirt, kicked up as long plumes of dust behind my van. This backcountry was empty of humanity, just the odd tin-roofed shed or grazing herd of steers. A series of tight switchbacks led me up 1,200 feet onto a main plateau, where showers had just washed the air, releasing the sweet, peppery scent of sage—that most western of smells. I drove through high meadows lush with grass and wildflowers, past slopes dark with the slim straight trunks of lodgepole pine. Only on moist, cool heights can such trees survive, well above the arid plains.

For all their peaceful appearance today, the Cypress Hills have had a bloody past. Long a hunting ground for the Blackfoot and other tribes, the region changed in the 1870s when white men began trading whiskey to the Indians. They might as well have sold them poison. An ugly series of confrontations ensued, culminating in the 1873 Cypress Hills Massacre, in which

Recruits parade smartly at "Depot" Division, the Royal Canadian Mounted Police Academy in Regina, Saskatchewan. Organized in 1873 during the frontier years, the first unit of Mounties, some 300 men, routed whiskey traders who preyed on Plains Indians. Present-day members enforce federal and provincial laws, and also serve as police in hundreds of small towns.

20 Indians were killed by drunken whites. The only bright spot in this story is the rise of the North-West Mounted Police, who patrolled the region and prosecuted all lawbreakers, white or red. The Mounties' monument in the Cypress Hills is Fort Walsh, a national historic park known as "the cradle of the Force."

Coming down from the hills, I drove through some of Canada's emptiest land, the plains of eastern Alberta. The road stretched ahead, ten miles without a curve, running over flat ground that bore only short grass dried to a dull yellow-brown. But "empty" is attractive to a stranger from crowded New Jersey; out here, I often drove into evening just to watch light fill up the land. On the far horizon sunset grew deep and angled, throwing the van's shadow back toward night. Light flared on every surface, from dark scuds of cloud to the feathered pink fronds of fox-tail barley. Whatever lay ahead, I thought, would suit me fine. On the wings of this good cheer I was searching *(Continued on page 130)*

High-stepping Cree Indian dances at Mosaic '86, Regina's annual Rainbow of Cultures celebration. Members of Indian bands, which today number nearly 600, and immigrant ethnic groups—from Scandinavians to Vietnamese—take part in the three-day event. Held in late spring, the festival honors Canada's multicultural heritage. Pavilions representing more than 20 cultures offer food, entertainment, and souvenirs. Concluding a day's activities, performers and audience members join in the Round Dance (below), symbolically sealing their friendship by holding hands. Tepees, drumbeats, and chanting help recall for the 35,000 visitors the days when Indians roamed the plains following bison herds.

Sediment from ancient rivers and centuries of erosion combined to create the badlands of Alberta's Dinosaur Provincial Park. A UNESCO World Heritage Site, the 15,000-acre park contains one of the richest deposits of Cretaceous fossils found anywhere. In the Red Deer River area (right), paleontologists drill into sandstone cliffs to expose the bones of centrosaurs, a type of horned dinosaur. Gilles Danis (above, at left) and Gerhard Maier painstakingly extract bones to be identified at the Tyrrell Museum of Palaeontology, in Drumheller.

for Alberta's badlands, located on the Red Deer River about 60 miles northwest of Medicine Hat. A local rancher directed me to turn at the next hamlet: "You watch Patricia close; it's not very big." Another eight or ten miles and the plains opened into a sudden gulf of strongly eroded forms: tall cones and fantasy castles, hoodoos with flat toadstool tops. The earth lay bared in tiers of color, sharply etched yet melting rapidly from rain and wind. This steady rate of erosion has exposed a scientific bonanza, the richest fossil digs in North America.

For several days I stayed in Dinosaur Provincial Park at the "paleo camp," a field research site administered by the Tyrrell Museum of Palaeontology in nearby Drumheller. The scientists and students at the camp are bent on exploring the Upper Cretaceous. In that era, 65 to 100 million years ago, Alberta lay at the edge of a warm shallow sea. Sharks and marine reptiles swam offshore, while giant dinosaurs roamed the humid tropical land. Dave Eberth, an expert on sediment layers, drove me into the badlands to explain what they told him: "We find most dinosaurs in old sand beds, the remains of rivers that flowed into the shallow sea 75 million years ago. Mudstone, rich with volcanic ash, is everywhere"—perhaps a clue to why the dinosaurs died so swiftly, still one of the great mysteries of paleontology.

Dave believes part of the answer lies here: "This park is the mecca for dinosaur fieldwork; with 35 species collected to date, we are close to rebuilding the animals' complex ecosystem. Eventually we'll know what they ate and where they traveled, the bugs that rode along." Deducing those patterns from geological evidence takes patience and long strides of imagination. Working beside the experts are volunteers who want to try some weeks of fieldwork. One evening Tyrrell Museum staff member Mike Klassen led a group of new arrivals out to see the bone beds, where excavation has slowly uncovered a dinosaur graveyard. "We've found remains of over 50 centrosaurs here. One theory is that a herd tried to cross the river and drowned." We crowded around a recent exposure of dark, fossilized bone: "You get at this stuff with hammers and chisels, then dental picks. Bones tell the animal's story—age, sex, diet, size." This was an adult thighbone, nearly three feet long.

Next morning, Mike and Kevin Aulenback reversed that scale by taking us to "micro-sites," where tiny bones and bone fragments have washed directly from the sand. "No one's invented an X ray for rock," Kevin said, "so you have to put your nose right on it." Soon the group was stretched out and intently probing with dental

picks. The day was cool and cloudy, conditions that Mike praised: "After a rain, wet bones shine and really stand out—Hey, look at this!" He had found a mammal tooth, only his second in six years of prospecting. Not to be outdone, I picked up a palm-size bone—what's this, bison? "Nope," said Kevin. "That's part of a dinosaur rib." One of the volunteers was getting feverish: "This place is a cathedral," he exclaimed.

To me the paleo camp was an outdoor university, with an international enrollment. A team of Chinese scholars was here to learn methods of excavation—and also the Western life-style. In camp one afternoon I gave Li Rong from Inner Mongolia an English lesson, writing out his answers to my simple questions: What is your favorite food? "My favorite food is . . . (much consulting of a dictionary) beef barbecue." Even so, the Chinese often cooked their own noodles and shrimp, which other diners happily downed as an extra course. At table I counted researchers from five Provinces, four States, and three other lands: a little nation of naturalists.

Most of this work ensues under the supervision of the Tyrrell Museum of Palaeontology. Opened in 1985, the museum has rapidly become a popular tourist attraction with its sound-and-light displays of dinosaur replicas, all fierce teeth and warty skin. Kids ogle these "monsters" and try out the hands-on exhibits. At computer

Boomtown excitement hits Calgary, Alberta, during the annual Exhibition and Stampede, a ten-day revival of the city's boisterous cow town past. Gleaming office buildings — Calgary is home to some 650 oil firms — soar above booths and exhibits crowding streets below. Seventy miles west of Calgary sprawl the majestic Canadian Rockies.

terminals they design their own dinosaurs, learning that an immense head needs a strong neck for support. Behind the scenes, technicians labor to assemble new exhibits and catalog more than 60,000 specimens, one of the world's largest and most diverse dinosaur collections.

From the paleo camp I returned to the Trans-Canada and drove 80 miles, passing sprawling cattle ranches and fields swept by sprinkler "rain" to reach Calgary, where the western plains end. Born as a cow town, Calgary boomed with later discoveries of rich oil and gas fields, the same elixir that flutters the pulse of its northern rival, Edmonton. Oil means an up-and-down economy, but still the stretch limos head for town every midsummer to celebrate the Calgary Exhibition and Stampede, fairly billed as the greatest Wild West show on earth. For ten days the city residents put on jeans and broad-brimmed hats to celebrate that fabled rootin'-tootin' past, when life was a big long roundup of broncs and steers, strong silent cowpokes and mighty pretty women.

Of course I bought a cowboy hat, also a chambray shirt and red bandanna; in this costume party I wouldn't play the dude. The Stampede begins with a mammoth downtown parade, which in three hours reprises the whole western story: Indians, trappers, homesteaders, and immigrants went by, many on horses or on decorated floats, accompanied by marching brass bands. The Canadian mosaic was passing, too: Chinese dragons and Filipino dancers, veiled Ismaili and turbaned Sikhs. The Stampede is a great party, but also a celebration of national purpose. And an opportunity to raise charity funds: "Be generous," loudspeakers implored "Our money-catchers are coming by."

Out at the Stampede Grounds, money was fast changing hands at the Frontier Casino, but the competition was friendlier among sheep-shearers and blacksmiths, the latter racing to shoe a pony in just ten minutes flat. I could also see races between horses, bison — and pigs. Four little pink Yorkshires trained by John Capobianco: "I trained 'em with Oreos. At the finish line I first put out four cookies, then cut it back three, two, one. They're all going for the same prize now, and you should see those trotters run!" I did, and the crowd went wild, cheering at the Stampede's first Pork Derby.

After 20 years of announcing the Stampede rodeo, Bill Kehler wears a satisfied grin: "I had two dreams, to be a cowboy and go on the radio, and rodeo lets me do both." As announcer, he keeps the show rolling, fills the lulls with gags, and explains the rules of competition. The only person working harder is a rodeo clown: "When a Brahma bull throws a rider, that clown has to step in and turn the bull away. That's 1,800 pounds full of fury; I'd rather face a saddle bronc any day. When you see a champion ride with his chest out and back straight, reaching with the spurs, you feel some thrill, I'll tell you. These boys wear no protection, and they take rougher shocks than football players. You get on, fall off, and ask why. If you're hearing answers you get aboard again. If not, you pick up a microphone."

That evening Bill was radio announcer for the chuck wagon races, an elaborate event in which teams of men, horses, and wagons clatter around the track for prize money totaling more than $260,000. I stood by an old-timer who seemed to know every rider and driver. Did he ever ride in these races? "No thanks. I got more sense than that." After the last event, I turned up my collar against the deep chill of a late July evening. Cold weather tonight, I remarked to the gent. "Oh yow, be snowball time before long. It's all from that big storm up in Banff last night." Tomorrow I would head for that realm of snow-wreathed peaks, far above the dry plains of central Canada.

Bucking competitions during the Stampede's daily rodeo—Canada's largest—draw participants of all ages. Twisted Sister tries hard to toss a bareback rider (above). Taking a not so wild and woolly ride, five-year-old Calvin Johansen (left) goes after a bronze buckle in the "mutton busting" contest.

FOLLOWING PAGES: Ridin' hell-bent-for-leather, whooping chuck wagon racers vie for stakes of more than $260,000. Though plagued by accidents in the past, the event remains the Stampede's most popular.

Mountain splendors of Alberta's Banff National Park provide the backdrop as outfitter Keith Robinson prepares lunch for guests during a six-day, 70-mile horse packing trip. Rainbow Lake mirrors slopes of the Vermilion Range. Such unspoiled spots exist throughout Canada's high country, which offers year-round recreation for hikers, skiers, canoeists, and other nature lovers.

OVER THE

HIGH COUNTRY

The Cordillera

I left Calgary at the start of August, on Heritage Day weekend, a holiday that launches the final days of Alberta's summer. Cars were streaming west on the Trans-Canada, filled with vacation-bound families. Mine, too: Bonnie was again at the wheel, and beside her rode our son, Jeff, monitoring the tape player. His sister, Jenny, had stayed home to work and pack for college. At 16, Jeff admired the ski jumps we passed at Canada Olympic Village, site of the 1988 Winter Games, but he was not about to swoon over new country. "Looks like Yellowstone," he said, as we climbed into foothills that rose before us in layered ridges of white spruce and aspen.

In the van's backseat I studied maps of our destination, the Canadian Rockies. Rearing up from the plains, the Rockies are North America's longest mountain range, sweeping 1,900 miles from British Columbia to New Mexico. They form the eastern edge of a vast cordillera that stretches along the Pacific coast, mountains borne upward by the same tectonic shocks that yield earthquakes and volcanoes. The Canadian Rockies are youthful, still rising from pressures that bend and break rock layers into heaped, jagged peaks—some more than 12,000 feet high. A perpetual arctic cold grips those heights, packing them with glacial ice fields. "Maybe you'll get in some August skiing," I told Jeff.

The road lifted steadily as we followed the Bow River and Canadian Pacific Railway tracks. Trains first reached this region in the 1880s, as part of the transcontinental rail link. Railway directors soon envisioned a passenger trade after the discovery of warm mineral springs at Banff. Mountain spas were popular in Europe; why not here as well? "Since we can't export the scenery," wrote one CPR official, "we'll have to import the tourists." Hotels sprang up at Banff—but only after property squabbles that led to the region's being declared Canada's first national park, in 1885. Today Banff and six adjacent parks in Alberta and British Columbia cover 8,900 square miles, Canada's largest mountain reserve.

On this holiday weekend, it seemed that half of Calgary's traffic followed us on the 80-mile journey to Banff. Cars, buses, and bikes slowly edged through town, while sidewalks thronged with crowds of tourists. Surrounded by high peaks, Banff plays resort host to more than three million visitors a year. Many of the patrons in local hotels and restaurants were Japanese, enjoying the strength of their currency. Signs and menus were multilingual; at dinner our waitress confided: "I know my foreign courtesy phrases; never hurts the tips."

For a taste of solitude I arose next dawn and walked along the Vermilion Lakes, a wetlands habitat for birds and moose. Only scattered geese moved on the still, flat waters, where mist lifted slowly to the rising sun. Light first touched the tops of flanking western peaks, then drew down their slopes in broad shafts of gold to reach the pooled water. The sky turned from lemon to pale blue; at dusk those hues would flame a deep rose-vermilion. For now the water was a perfect sky-mirror, inverting the forest fringe in long, dark streaks of spruce.

Next I roused the family for a morning dip at Cave and Basin Centennial Centre, where hot mineral water endlessly bubbles forth from its long journey through the earth. We lightly cooked in an outdoor swimming pool, then adjourned to the teahouse for pots of brew and raspberry tarts. The warm springs affect this entire slope of Sulphur Mountain, creating an environment rarely seen in northern montane regions. Orchids and sunflowers bloom along the pool's runoff stream, which flows into a marsh. Some of the robins and ducks there never migrate, living through long winters in steamy comfort. In the shallows dart tropical fish, probably released years ago from home aquariums.

From that thriving scene we drove to nearby Bankhead, a ghost town that once mined coal for the Canadian Pacific Railway. The seams here

Known collectively as the Canadian Cordillera, the mountain ranges of western Alberta and eastern British Columbia—Rockies, Purcells, and Selkirks—challenged the Trans-Canada's builders. Roads here traverse a dramatic landscape of snowy peaks, glacier-carved valleys, alpine meadows, and dense woodlands—much of it preserved in some two dozen national or provincial parks.

yielded semianthracite, ancient plants transformed by 140 million years of decay and pressure. This coal is hard but brittle; heaps of discarded slack still lie among the site's black, cindery walkways. In its heyday, 1904 to 1922, Bankhead produced a thousand tons of coal a day and sported the modern comforts of electric lights and a curling rink. Now we could only imagine the town, aided by plaques set amid crumbled walls and rusting machinery. Today's residents are a colony of plump Columbian ground squirrels. They live in the slack heaps, digging tunnel mazes like a race of tiny, determined miners.

Returning to the Trans-Canada, we pulled off to make an evening tour of Banff's "buffalo paddock," a hundred acres of fenced woodland habitat for bison. Warned by signs to remain in the van, we drove at a creeping pace along the paved circuit, studying every dark, bulky shape in the trees. No bison. At the gate I met Tracy Thornton, a summer employee hired to study visitor usage of the paddock. "This is an old, popular attraction in the park; it draws over 120,000 visitors a year." But where are the bison? "Tonight they're lying down in some low spots. You can see them if you go really slow—I clocked your trip at six minutes."

At dawn next morning, Tracy put her car into a terrapin crawl while Nora Kopjar, the project supervisor, explained their work: "We have a small herd of wood bison here; just four cows, three calves, and a bull. Sam went out roaming last May, but now he's back for the rut—and to feed with his girls." Why are they so hard to see? "Wood bison are larger than plains bison, but more resourceful. They forage both in the open and under trees, and for huge animals they blend well into cover. If they're just five feet into the woods, you can't see them."

Hence we saw nothing on our first circuit, a reminder of how elusive bison have become. Once herds of perhaps 60 million thundered

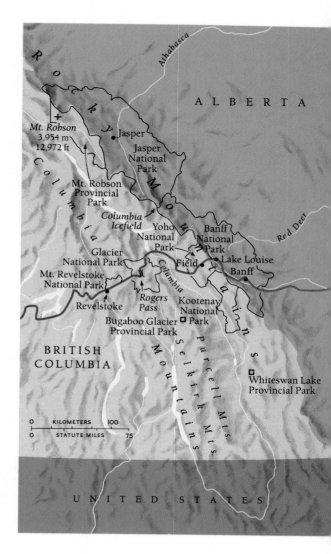

across North America, but a century of hunting with horses and guns reduced the population to a mere thousand by 1890. Protected enclosures and breeding programs have brought the animals back from near-extinction, but they will never again achieve their old numbers. "Lots of buffalo trees in there today," said Tracy, as we began a second tour. "Some days I stop and look at the same trees or shadows 12 times. I get skunked exactly 26 percent of the time."

Tracy and Nora keep these figures for a Trans-Canada Highway project designed to lessen the road's impact on park wildlife. "Fences along the park highway have reduced the number of road kills," Nora said, "but the animals can't move between their spring and winter ranges. We may have to relocate this paddock to improve elk movement. Other options are to modify the paddock or remove the bison." As rain began to fall Tracy let out a whoop, and suddenly we saw two bison cows emerge from the gloom. They were browsing on shrubs, ten leaves to a gulp, and close behind followed a calf. "That's PJ, our firstborn," Nora smiled. "I named him for my thesis supervisor."

Tracy had the same affection for Sam, who soon appeared with a swing of his massive head. "What a big guy he is; with that nice beard hanging down and those huge front quarters." Weighing well over a ton, Sam dwarfed our car; his shaggy chest and shoulders rolled with an easy, brute strength. He was eight years old; with luck and winter feed, he would reach 20 or 30. Tracy jotted some notes and charted positions on her map. "If we have to move the paddock," she said, "we need to know where and when the bison are most visible. People do want to see them. Here I've been looking at these animals all summer, and they're still fascinating."

More absorbing to Jeff was the lure of a top Canadian golf course at the Banff Springs Hotel. This towering 800-room castle succeeded a smaller hotel built here by the CPR in 1888, a

Former Olympian Dave Irwin lifts off during a run at Sunshine Village in Banff National Park, host to three million visitors annually. Copious snowfall and a six-month season boost the region's winter appeal.

FOLLOWING PAGES: Banff townsite, on the Bow Valley floor, recedes beneath summit-bound competitors at Mount Norquay ski area.

structure later destroyed by fire. Today's hotel provides its guests with baronial opulence in a wilderness setting. After a day's round of touring, diners sup in medieval halls with vaulted ceilings and carved oak panels. Jeff steered me to the golf course, a par-71 that stretches along the Bow River. For thousands of years this high mountain meadow was a peace grounds for the Plains Indians, a place where tribes met amiably in summer and traded goods. Beneath the first tee lie the remains of sundance lodges, the scene of sacred hunting rites.

Today the course was full of Sunday hackers, mixed foursomes in casual togs. The rules of play were also relaxed, for who could compete in this scenery? Grassy fairways spread away, dotted with smooth greens and well-groomed bunkers. We crossed the river and walked out along a public road, shadowed by snow-rimmed peaks. Jeff studied a score card, playing each hole with imaginary strokes. He was two over par as we reached the No. 8 tee, a Rocky Mountain classic: the ball had to drive across a deep gorge and then hook left to avoid the massive, 9,600-foot upsweep of Mount Rundle. The tee was empty; Jeff stepped up, gripped a phantom club, and sent a perfect shot winging on its way.

At Banff we left the Trans-Canada for the parallel Bow Valley Parkway, less crowded but slower because of its many turnouts, places to pull aside and admire mountain views. We were crossing from the younger Front Ranges, rock twisted into many-folded layers, to the older Main Ranges, which soar in massive uplift. They present columned and crowned expanses of barren gray stone, with belts of dark forest below. The summits have choppy, serrated edges, like knife blades thrust to the sky, and the lower slopes spread out to form broad temple pyramids. On both sides these ranges loomed up, until we seemed to be sailing down a long corridor lined by giant sea vessels.

Rowboats and canoes plied the waters of Lake Louise, home of the famous hotel built by the Canadian Pacific Railway. Lake Louise is a luxury resort with bygone standards of comfort: boating on the lake, hiking along extensive wooded trails that lead to shelters and teahouses. Visitors stroll a few miles, then stop for an afternoon crumpet. Most prefer the lakefront promenade and its view of Mount Victoria on the opposite shore, a rearing, snow-crowned massif that rises in a series of sharp V-cut defiles. On calm days the lake presents a striking hourglass pattern of angular ridges, all mirrored in pale ice-blue water.

The Trans-Canada turns west at Lake Louise, but to see the Rockies fully we headed north on the Icefields Parkway. This 145-mile road is one of the world's great mountain drives, winding through high passes and along a succession of dazzling glacial icefields, the frozen rooftop of the Great Divide. The snowmelt here flows north, east, and west across the continent, finally to reach the Arctic, Atlantic, and Pacific Oceans. We saw that process beginning at Peyto Lake, where glacial runoff forms a broad expanse of rippling turquoise water. The color comes from "rock flour," fine particles of crushed bedrock that reflect blue and green light.

A side road carried us up to Bow Summit, where several foot trails lead to upper elevations. While Bonnie perused the alpine flowers, Jeff and I decided to walk "just a little higher." We moved along an easy ascent, pausing to survey the valley opening out behind us. Its broad U-shaped contour was obvious, the form plowed by a moving ice pack. Near us rose a 12-story-high moraine, gravel dumped by retreating walls of melting ice. Those processes occurred more than 20,000 years ago, but since then vegetation has only slowly recovered on the mountaintops. We passed tree line, saw flowers give way to

moss and lichens, and still the trail led upward. As we rested, a lone hiker appeared—heading down. "Oh, I'm glad to meet someone," she said. "I saw a lot of fresh bear signs just a way back." Why, of *course* we'd walk her down.

Bonnie drove north slowly, for we often stopped at turnouts to take in the panorama of Canada's high country. The Icefields Parkway follows valleys cut by fast-rushing rivers, braided streams that part and meet around shifting gravel bars, and above them rear mountains of colossal height and girth. More than once Jeff endured our exclamation, "Look, look at the rock!" Plied with light and shadow, the Rockies take on ever-shifting forms. Strong vertical palisades give way to flat-topped mesas, then castles appear with pillars and peaked turrets. On the high slopes, snow lies in crevices and ledges, and higher still rise the glaciers, great masses of compacted ice.

The heart of glacier country is the 125-square-mile Columbia Icefield, which straddles the Divide and two national parks, Banff and Jasper. We crossed into Jasper and stopped at Icefield Chalet, a red-roofed building opposite the foot of Athabasca Glacier. Travelers were pulling in for food, gas, and maps; from there they could take backcountry hikes or—a popular alternative—ride in motorized "snocoaches" up onto the glacial surface. I wanted to go higher and look out over the entire Icefield, preferably by hiking. "Take the Wilcox Pass Trail," a park warden advised. "And don't forget to carry water and carbohydrates."

We camped that evening at Wilcox Creek, one of many public campgrounds provided in the Rockies. After pancakes next morning we hit the trail, moving quickly up cool, shaded slopes until reaching a sharp upward ascent. For a good half hour we labored on, tripping on exposed roots and slippery moss. During one rest, Bonnie read from a pamphlet: " 'The first section of the trail is relatively steep.' Well, at least they warned us." Until 1930 or so Wilcox Pass was a main route around Athabasca Glacier, which used to block the lower valley. Outfitters led horse and mule trains up here; we should be able to make it. "Need some mountain goat blood," muttered Jeff, who was already into the carbohydrates.

On we scrambled, following sharp switchbacks that eased the grade slightly, until we broke from trees and came into sunshine. Cars crawled by on the parkway below; up here we paced through a rolling alpine meadow, abloom with tall stands of pink-spired fireweed and golden asters. Shrubs grew thick and stubby, the effect of long exposure to snow and cold winds. We came to a racing stream, the water welling in a smooth blue pool before plunging down 80-foot cliffs. Birds clung to this wet, green haven; we scared off a golden eagle, which may have been eyeing a plump ptarmigan. Oblivious of us, it busily pecked at a stand of dark red mountain cranberries. Color was the bird's guardian: now the speckled gray-brown of rocks, it would turn pure white by snowfall.

Revived by this easy walking, Jeff moved ahead to scout for a view facing the Icefield. His blue jacket disappeared over a ridgeline, and when we got there he had dropped from sight. A flutter of concern arose: ahead lay a deep ravine, which the trail avoided with a long detour to the right. If he took the trail, we should still see him. Did he find a cutoff . . . "or fall into a crevice?" said his mother. We fanned out, with me searching the ravine. No Jeff. I climbed a crest and found alpine gardens, the low cushion plants with tiny blooms of pale yellow and rose red. Ahead lay Wilcox Pass, a mile-wide avenue between two mountains. In all that immensity of sky, rock, and snow, I saw no blue jacket.

Following a trail marked by cairns, I rejoined Bonnie near a small depression, one befitting our mood. We had sunshine now, but

clouds were blowing in from the west. Afternoon was coming on; when darkness or mist reached the pass, it would be impossible to conduct a hunt. As we scanned all horizons a figure emerged near some distant boulders and approached us. We greeted Hugh Murray, a teacher from Vancouver. Had he seen our son? "He passed me a while ago; said you should meet up on that ridge. And to hurry; he's starving."

Up there Hugh joined us for sandwiches followed by fruit and chocolate, and we all ate with outdoor appetites. In bright sun, the air at 8,000 feet was cool and dry; a brisk wind kept our jackets on. From this lower slope of Mount Wilcox we looked beyond Athabasca Glacier to its source in the Columbia Icefield, an expanse of gleaming ivory that rose in heaps to the west and north. A frequent hiker of the Rockies, Hugh examined our large-scale map of this area. "We're seeing only one arm of the Icefield; it spreads along the Divide and flows into all these lower valleys." Each valley glacier formed a broad descending river of ice, pulled downward by its weight yet also melting in retreat.

On our return through Wilcox Pass, Hugh pointed to damp patches of sedge and rush: "Those wet spots were the last snowbanks to melt. The plants get only a few weeks to bloom and seed before snow returns." Winter also brings high winds and bitter cold to the mountains, yet many forms of life survive here. Coming down we saw pikas and marmots, rodents that live where people rarely go. At our approach the air filled with sharp, warning squeaks and whistles. Moving ahead as usual, Jeff suddenly stopped: Four bighorn sheep came over a rise and browsed toward us. A ram and three ewes, they bore thick curling horns ridged with growth rings. The ram passed within 20 feet of me, close enough to count seven years on his battered headgear.

Late that day we visited Athabasca, one of the world's few glaciers reached by car. Close up,

the mere "toe" of this behemoth dwarfed the hundreds of ant-people climbing on its broad surface. We passed signs marking recessional moraines, the masses of gravel dumped by melting ice. In retreat a glacier most reveals its power, pulling back from rubble that was once a mountaintop. Slowly the glacier had bulldozed its way to this terminus, a three-mile journey that took 150 years. At the base a wide, roaring stream now rushed forth, meltwater from channels deep within. The ice was pale blue, and its wet surface chilled the air. Carefully avoiding crevasses, Jeff and I climbed a steep, slushy path up the toe. We looked down the tilting grade and had the same thought: skiing in August. With a quick downhill slide, he beat me to the bottom.

On a hazy morning we drove north along the Icefields Parkway, past braided river channels hung with a fine gray mist. This water would follow an intricate drainage system to the Arctic Ocean, 2,200 miles distant. Our destination was the town of Jasper, where the Parkway ends and we would begin a return loop. Far less crowded than Banff, Jasper provides an outpost for backpackers bound on wilderness trips. Many shops sell camping equipment, while others post advisories: "No food, pets, or packs inside, please." We opted for a picnic at Patricia Lake, one of dozens of glacial ponds surrounding the town. The blue-emerald water was warm in its sunstruck shallows, but frigid out deep. One swimmer braved the cold; his arm strokes cut long, smooth V-wakes on the glassy surface.

Equally placid were the evening visitors at Wapiti Campground, about 30 brown, white-rumped elk moving serenely through campsites. Astonished diners froze, forks in midair, as the animals browsed near picnic tables. Wapiti, as elk were called by the Cree, are common in the Rockies but not always so tame. They were

Cosmopolitan flavor prevails at the Banff Springs Hotel, where chef Sakae Kuratani of the Samurai Sushi Bar displays an artful sampling of sashimi, Japanese-style raw fish. Numerous eating and greeting spots, shops, and sports facilities draw visitors from around the world for a taste of civilization's refinements at wilderness's edge.

enjoying a quiet phase in their year-long cycle, late summer before the fall rut begins. The herd was all cows and calves, for bulls remain apart. By September they would begin to gather cow harems, challenging other bulls with a call that resembles a high, clear bugle solo. That wild sound has a plaintive note, for elk now occupy less than 10 percent of their original North American range. They had a prior claim on Wapiti Campground, and not in name alone.

Turning south, we headed back to the Trans-Canada and stopped near Mount Kerkeslin for an interesting sight, two mountain goats by the highway. A nanny and her kid had come down from timberline to nibble in the roadside clay, a source of salt and minerals. Just a tiny ball

of white fluff, the kid rested quietly while Mom rooted in the dirt. She needed the nutrients to replace those lost in molting, an annual process that sheds her thick, cream-white coat. Now in a short summer trim, by October she would regain cold-weather attire and return to the usual habitat of high cliffs and grassy ledges, beyond most predators. Ever wary, she ushered her kid across the road and down a slope to a hiding place.

On the road we often saw touring cyclists, mostly young people with the stamina to pedal up mountain grades. They dressed lightly, just shorts and tank tops, with helmets and knee pads for safety. I stopped to talk with René Rich, a solo rider who was taking landscape photos. A college student from Colorado, she believes in

Water naturally warmed to a care-melting 100°F shakes the chill off a March day for Melanie McGilvery, relaxing in Lussier Hot Spring in Whiteswan Lake Provincial Park. Thermal features abound in the region; their discovery at Banff by railroad workers in 1883 led to creation of the national park.

the strenuous life: "I'm a major in outdoor rec, so this is how I spend vacations! My trip is all national parks: I started out in Yellowstone, then Glacier, now Banff and Jasper. This leg will take about eight days, but that's because I stay in hostels and go hiking." Do many people ride solo? "I meet quite a few. It's okay if you like being on your own—and can fix bikes. The road is good here; I make about 50 miles a day and really see the country. This place is burning up my film!"

At Lake Louise we regained the Trans-Canada and turned west to cross the Great Divide. The road climbed the Alberta side, peaked at 5,329 feet and then plummeted down into British Columbia. We had entered Yoho National Park via Kicking Horse Pass. "Yoho" is a Cree word expressing awe and wonderment, which is probably what James Hector felt in 1858 when his trusty horse walloped him in the chest. Hector was the first geologist to explore and map this pass, willing horse or no, and his expedition opened a long search for a land route between the prairies and the Pacific coast. In return for joining Canada in 1871, British Columbia eventually got its railway link to Montreal, built at enormous cost through Kicking Horse Pass.

Bonnie instinctively hit the brakes as we descended Big Hill, once the steepest rail grade in North America. The highway rides atop the old CPR track bed, dropping 1,300 feet in only six miles. This 4 percent incline caused so many runaway trains and accidents that in 1909 engineers replaced the tracks and halved the grade with a pair of spiral tunnels. Mile-long freight trains come pounding through this looping figure-eight "pretzel," their locomotives exiting long before cabooses enter. Passenger trains also cross here daily, many with domed observation cars for viewing the Rockies. But autos and trucks provide the main access today, since completion of the Trans-Canada Highway.

We saw the effects of that traffic on Yoho by taking a brief detour down the Emerald Lake

Road. Near a marshy spot about 30 vehicles had parked; the owners had their cameras trained on two moose, a cow and a calf. The hushed crowd had gathered reverently around these creatures to record some guzzling of springwater. Amid shutter clicks, the cow sucked at a mineral spring while fending off Junior. Finally she moved away and he timidly came to the pool. Because his neck was short he knelt on his forelegs to take a long draft. The clicks rose in chorus, like a host of cicadas.

After camping overnight in Yoho, we doubled back across the Divide to enter Kootenay National Park, also in British Columbia. Yoho and Kootenay belong to the Rockies' Western Main Range, mountains less eroded than those in Banff and Jasper. Its distance from the Trans-Canada gives Kootenay a respite from heavy tourist traffic. We saw few visitors on the trail in Marble Canyon, a narrow gorge of smooth gray limestone washed with blue glacial water. At points the canyon sides lay so close that squirrels could jump across. The rim was hot and sunny, with bees humming in sweet clover, while the stream below frothed in a cool, misty grotto, worn by eons of rushing water. Ahead of us, Jeff Lawrence was intently studying some flowers. A botanist? "Hydrologist. I work in Denver and do research on groundwater all over the West. This is just a vacation trip; they're not worried about water quality here."

Nearby lay Paint Pot Trail, where the Kootenay and Stony nations once came for war paint. The oxidized earth made good tepee and house paint, too, so later entrepreneurs mined the site until 1916. Some rusting machinery remains, along with unshipped mounds of bright orange-red dirt. Atop a hill stand three paint pots, formations that accumulate around mineral springs. Over the years iron deposits build up

in layered rings, creating a caldron with raised edges. Inside, green water wells up and spills down the hillside in streams of bright rust. I followed the red water downhill till it merged with a blue creek. The Indians feared and revered this place, believing it ruled by the thunder spirit.

We drove south in Kootenay through the variable weather of mountains, passing from sunshine to brief showers. Clouds billowed above ridges like puffs of volcano smoke, while light shone in silvery patches on the dark, spreading forest below. British Columbia holds one-fourth of North America's commercial timber, enough to guarantee that *these* trees will never face harvest. While the Canadian parks may have begun with motives for profit, today they exist mainly to preserve the incalculable resource of wildness. Someone captured that idea on a sign at the park's south entrance: "The Mountains Shall Bring Peace to the People."

At Radium Hot Springs we turned north for Golden, a 65-mile ride along part of the Rocky Mountain Trench, one of the world's longest continuous valleys. Possibly a rift formation, the trench runs 900 miles along the eastern margin of British Columbia. We ran beside the upper Columbia River, a stripling version of the mighty course that flows through Idaho and Washington to reach the Pacific. Once salmon battled their way to these headwaters, an astounding journey through 1,200 miles of fast currents and cascades. In the early 1800s Golden was a fur trade center, providing access for rafts and boats to the far-distant Pacific. Now hydroelectric dams have penned the river into long reservoir lakes, without fish or boats to be seen.

West of Golden, the Trans-Canada lifted us into Glacier National Park and the Selkirk Mountains, a range of metamorphic rock. Older and tougher than the Rockies, the Selkirks have eroded slowly into craggy spires, many covered with permanent ice. Glaciers top more than 400 peaks in the park, or 12 percent of its 520 square miles. Even in mid-August the 11,000-footers shine with a thick white frosting, for the region is a snow trap. Prevailing winds pick up warm, moist air from the Pacific and dump it here as snow, up to 60 feet a year. On the highest slopes that load can only move one way, cascading downward in enormous avalanches.

We entered the narrow, twisting gap of Rogers Pass, the most avalanche-prone section of Glacier. Ahead lay a 15-mile stretch that forms a battle zone during each winter's "Snow Wars." At strategic emplacements, Royal Canadian Horse Artillery teams set up 105mm howitzers and fire rounds to bring down controlled snowslides. Once loosened, the snow runs a gamut of rubble mounds and earthen dams that slow or deflect its descent, finally spilling harmlessly across the highway and its protective snowsheds. But these concrete structures, some nearly half a mile long, do not always protect highway travelers. Often the winter storms rage for days and slide conditions are out of control. "When that happens," Fred Schleiss told me, "we shut the highway down. In 1972 we closed for nine days straight."

From his headquarters in Rogers Pass, Fred has directed the Glacier avalanche defense since 1959, sharing the duties with his brother, Walter, and a Parks Canada crew. They face some of the most hazardous snow conditions on earth: "Glacier has the combination of heavy snow pack and steep terrain in a national traffic corridor, the number one highway and railroad. Last February over 90 avalanches hit Rogers Pass in a 24-hour period. Some were dusters, but they can push a railway car right off its tracks."

Fred has witnessed thousands of avalanches. "Some slides begin with a sharp, cracking sound, as the top layer breaks away from the pack and begins to fall. It's a bluish-white snow,

and on steep slopes it roars like a gun exploding. I've seen it fall a mile in a matter of seconds—close to 150 miles per hour."

A major avalanche can crush all obstacles in its path. "In 1981 one hit a 250-ton bridge and knocked it off its piers; it took crews three days—at a million dollars a day—to restore the bridge for traffic." At those prices, avalanche defense is a bargain. Each shell fired costs $500, and Fred keeps a healthy arsenal stockpiled for the long storms of winter. Snowfalls fluctuate over time, but he maintains a forecaster's perspective. "My philosophy is that every year can be bad."

Yet his work has clearly saved property and lives: Only two avalanche deaths have occurred since 1962, as contrasted with 240 in the decades before control began. Today the greatest hazard in Rogers Pass is to mountain hikers, who may come across unexploded rounds. "Once a soldier found a shell and left it *inside* a snow-measuring station, with all the telemetry equipment. He thought he was doing us a big favor."

At the Rogers Pass summit we stopped the van at a simple monument, two intersecting arches that mark the opening of the Trans-Canada Highway in 1962. Traffic has increased 400 percent since then; today much of it was heading west, toward Vancouver. We then sped down the road another 15 miles through Mount Revelstoke, last of the mountain national parks. The highway rapidly descended, passing from flower-strewn alpine meadows to the dark, dense interior rain forest of lower elevations.

We had entered logging and sawmill country, big trees stacked beside conical kilns. At Malakwa, the young woman pumping gas looked quite ready to handle a chain saw. With a glance at our license plate, she asked: "You from Seattle?" No, that's Washington, *D.C.* "Oh, to me Washington is just the first State south. Well D.C., have a good time in B.C.!" I was beginning to like it already.

Ice-etched landscapes lend majesty to Jasper, largest of the high country's national parks. At left, Columbia Glacier spreads from the Columbia Icefield, a 125-square-mile area where some 30 glaciers and three major river systems—bound for three oceans—originate. Starting more than a million years ago, the glaciers helped shape Jasper's features, including mile-high Maligne Lake and the brooding mountains of the Front Ranges (below).

FOLLOWING PAGES: Crenellated peaks frame Lake O'Hara; glacial silt tinges these waters a luminous turquoise. The lake and adjacent lodge, accessible only by permit, lie in British Columbia's Yoho National Park. A medley of mountains, lakes, and waterfalls inspired the park's name—from a Cree exclamation of awe and wonder.

"Snow Wars" pit howitzer-wielding artillerymen against a mountain nemesis—the avalanche—just west of Glacier National Park. Before danger mounts, mortar shells break up unstable snow pack; some 60 feet of snow annually makes this stretch of the Trans-Canada, over 4,300-foot-high Rogers Pass, vulnerable to slides. Another preventive measure, a concrete snowshed (below), channels slides over the roadway. Despite these and other defenses, slide conditions can still close the highway for days at a time (above).

Rumbling through a wintry landscape, trains follow parallel tracks west of Rogers Pass. The Trans-Canada breached the pass in 1962, some 70 years after the railroad arrived. "Such a view! Never to be forgotten!" wrote an 1881 explorer. At right, a climber ascends to similar views in Bugaboo Glacier Provincial Park. Snowpatch Spire stands sentinel at rear.

FOLLOWING PAGES: Horse packers skirt frothing Emperor Falls in Mount Robson Provincial Park. Nearby, the park's namesake peak crowns Canada's Rockies, and the Fraser River begins its meandering journey to the Pacific.

Spinnakers swell with the wind as yachts knife through the Strait of Juan de Fuca off Vancouver Island. During the Swiftsure Lightship Classic, some 150 boats race from Victoria to Swiftsure Bank and back. Life-styles focus on the outdoors in the scenic Pacific realm, where mountains, rain-swept forests, and a bounty of offshore islands combine for a rare diversity of climate and landscapes.

TOWARD

JOURNEY'S END

The Pacific Realm

As we descended into lower British Columbia, my thoughts ran ahead to the Pacific coast, where the Trans-Canada ends. The final leg of this long national road crosses a plateau and a mountain range to end on Vancouver Island, the western Mile 0. That route traverses a big country, but only a small part of British Columbia. Much of the province is roadless, especially in the wilderness that runs 800 miles north to the Yukon. With its 366,000 square miles, British Columbia encompasses more land than California, Oregon, and Washington combined. On this western rim of Canada, glacial peaks overlook warm coastal beaches, and small farms lie just beyond great harbor cities. Coming at my journey's end, B.C. summed up everywhere I had traveled.

The Columbia Mountains had been cool, with early signs of fall, but now the highway led us down to the central plateau, where summer lingered on. Caught in a rain shadow behind the coastal mountains, this sunny land is cut by fast-moving rivers that rush south from the heights, bearing snowmelt to the Pacific. Many streams have etched broad valleys that impound the run-off in finger lakes, brimful of water in dry country. With irrigation, the fertile lakeside slopes have bloomed into orchards and vineyards, perched above beach resorts. "Resorts?" said Jeff, "as in golf . . . tennis . . . and room service?" After weeks of camping, we turned south to seek a little comfort in the Okanagan Valley.

One possibility lay at Sicamous, "houseboat capital of Canada," where hundreds of floating homes rest on an arm of Shuswap Lake. That was a leisurely way to tour and fish, but we drove on. The road ran beside sailboats and water-skiers, and for a while we clocked a thin maroon speedboat at 60 miles per hour before it sped on by. The lake gave way to a winding river, lined with shade trees and open pastures. Dairy cows lounged in the midday heat, munching their way to milk time. We soon passed the milk's destination, a busy cheese factory in Armstrong. Beyond lay long, sinuous Okanagan Lake, a 70-mile reach lit by cloudless blue sky.

Rolling south toward Kelowna, I thought of Italian lakes and hills. Here the upper slopes were that same tawny gold, miles of dried grass topped with dark ridgelines of forest. Near the water spread irrigated fields, bright green and laid out in terraced symmetry. Roadside garden centers were selling "prairie hardy" plants, guaranteed drought-resistant. The annual rainfall here is barely 8 to 12 inches, but pipelines have turned the valley into a northwestern fruit bowl. Each year the Okanagan region produces a third of Canada's apples, half its pears and prunes, and all of its apricots—along with huge crops of peaches, cherries, and wine grapes.

Kelowna became our home base as we explored the lower valley. One morning Bonnie and I drove south along Okanagan Lake, through country that some locals call "the California of Canada." For several miles the Coyote Canal flowed beside us, an aqueduct dappled with bathers floating in rafts and inner tubes. Small towns went by—Peachland, Summerland, Penticton—each a farming community that later branched into selling sunshine vacations and retirement homes. Stands lined the road, offering peaches, nectarines, and every variety of berries.

Below Penticton, the valley narrows again to streams and small lakes that run on to the U.S. border. We halted at the village of Oliver and spent some hours with Denis Fleming, who superintends a fruit-packing plant for local growers. He walked us through rooms of silent machinery, about to crank up for apple harvest. "Next week, this will be one busy place—apples come floating down those troughs, go through a computer check for color, then get sized and sorted." Every apple shipped has a glossy polish and a sweet aroma: "I always notice the smell of first apples, but then it gets sort of common."

To show us why, Denis rolled back a heavy

Dropping down from the high country, the Trans-Canada enters a series of verdant north-to-south valleys. The road then runs through spectacular canyons etched by the Fraser River before rolling west to the Pacific shores, home to nearly half of the province's three million people. At Vancouver, ferries cross the Strait of Georgia, joining the mainland road to the final stretch of highway on Vancouver Island.

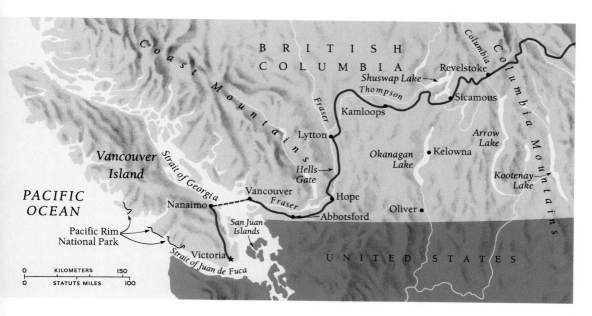

door and we stepped into December. A stream of 31°F air gusted over the cold storage room and its wooden bins of fruit: fresh 'cots and nectarines, last year's apples. Long-term storage has changed the industry, Denis explained: "We can now sell fresh packs year-round, and that means steady jobs for the plant workers." If only fruit ranching were as steady, I remarked. "You aren't kidding. The grower has to fight weather, disease, and bugs. Our problem is mainly the customer, who won't tolerate a bruise or blemish."

On his upland orchard, Ken Ziebart smiled at this description. "I worked in the packing house a few years, and the people problems made my stomach churn. Now I've got just one boss to please," he said, looking at his wife, Carole. She laughed, "Yes, but I'd like to have 25 cents for every trip you make to the orchard!" In late afternoon we sat on their patio overlooking 20 acres of fruit trees that sloped away in broad, leafy aisles. Apples had reached the late stage of ripening, as clusters of fruit began to turn gold and red. On neighboring land, sprinklers

pivoted in slow circles. Despite this scene of harvest bounty, Ken had an eye cocked for disaster.

"Every night we sit out here, look up at the mountain, and say 'Is this the time we're going to get it?'" Behind Mount Kobau lies the Similkameen Valley, where hot air rises and cools into what the Ziebarts call "monster clouds." Bad weather rips down this slope so often that crop failure comes as no surprise. "We lost our first two cherry crops to hard, pouring rain, the kind that splits fruit," said Ken. "The wind can sweep over the mountain and flatten our trees in a minute. But hail is the worst; in six years we've had three storms, and one wiped out the apples. The stones fell like bullets; on just one small McIntosh I counted 40 hits."

Carole grew up in Victoria, a city girl who bought apples mainly at supermarkets. But after marrying Ken she suggested that they move back to the Okanagan, his boyhood home. "My Mum worries sick about us and our 'pioneer life' out here. I tease her, 'Oh, next week we may be living in a tent,' and then she can't sleep at night."

Fertile countryside of the lower Fraser River Valley cradles a dairy
located two miles off the highway near Abbotsford. Snow-clad Mount Baker,
rising 10,778 feet in Washington's Cascades, commands the distant slopes.
Small towns and hundreds of farms checker the scenic valley, which
stretches 85 miles southeast from Vancouver.

Carole splits her time as a hospital dietitian and vegetable gardener. Her large plot bursts with corn and potatoes, carrots, beans, peas, and fat red tomatoes—a year's food for their family of five. "Ken's grandmother saw me weeding in the heat and said, 'Why that's the way I started, 60 years ago!' There's progress for you."

Bonnie and I drove home through sunset, going north along the shores of Okanagan Lake. The air blew hot against my arm, measuring a day that went into the 90s. All this orchard land was sagebrush a century ago, before settlers began to tap mountain lakes and drain irrigation water to the lower slopes. Pumping water up from Okanagan Lake was too expensive; it

remains a habitat for fishing and boating—and perhaps for Ogopogo, the region's legendary monster, a huge serpent with sheeplike head.

In the plateau region, most highway routes follow the winding course of river valleys. To reach the Trans-Canada again we threaded our way northwest to Kamloops, a city on the Thompson River. Major rivers in this region bear the names of early explorers: David Thompson, Simon Fraser, Alexander Mackenzie—Canadians who opened northwestern lands well before Lewis and Clark. In 1793 Mackenzie reached the Pacific "by Canada," as he wrote on a shoreline rock, after crossing extremely rugged terrain 400 miles north of Kamloops. Thompson made his

extensive southern journeys in 1804-12, mainly to open fur-trading posts.

Today the Thompson River Valley has largely turned to cattle ranching. The scant rainfall in this dry belt supports an open range of bunchgrass and sagebrush, spiked with prickly pear cactus. West of Kamloops we passed steers grazing on parched land; others rested on the riverbanks beneath shade trees. The earth looked hard and wrinkled, baked in pale shades of brown and tan beneath a metallic blue sky. Some slopes had that odd feature of western grasslands, corduroy ridges in a horizontal pattern. Legend says they came from "side-hill gougers," beasts that walked the hills on four legs, the uphill pair shorter than the other. Cattlemen note that herds do graze along the slopes, instead of up and down.

Near Ashcroft, the highway clung to the Thompson River as it began to cut steadily downward into the plateau. Backlit by sun, the river sparkled in bright platinum, its edges lashed with froth. Above us, treeless cliffs descended to broad flat benches, silt terraces that sometimes bore irrigated fields of alfalfa. Much of the exposed rock had a strong green tint, the verdigris sign of copper. Soon the river accelerated into a foaming raceway, as it tilted steeply down into Thompson Canyon. We had reached some of the fastest white water in western Canada, home of the river runners at Spences Bridge.

From April to October, several rafting companies offer float trips on the Thompson. The one-day run from Spences Bridge to Lytton negotiates 25 major rapids, including the ominously named Washing Machine and Jaws of Death. Thousands of thrill seekers take this ride each season, lining up to sign liability releases and don required life vests. We joined such a group one morning, along with a British family named Micklewright. I asked about their surname; what exactly was a Micklewright? "Probably a tinker," Bruce Micklewright said. "A wright is a maker, a mickle something small. There's an old saying, 'Takes many a mickle to make a muckle'—or, little things add up."

Bruce and his wife, Harriet, add up considerable travel mileage each year, since he flies for an airline based in Hong Kong, while she maintains their family home east of London. "We decided to meet halfway, in North America," she smiled. "It's our first trip here all together." Their two children were clearly excited about rafting. Though Emma maintained a calm befitting her 17 years, John, at 8, was more apprehensive: "Do you think we'll get wet?" he kept asking.

We shoved off, three rafts carrying about 50 passengers, making patches of bright silver and orange against the dark river current. For a while we drifted slowly in flat water, as our guide, Barry Burko, delivered instructions. Above him the Trans-Canada traffic sped by, and then two lines of railway cars, on opposite banks: "Stereo trains," he noted, as engineers from the CP and CN Railways exchanged courtesy blasts.

Unlike my two previous vessels in Canadian rapids, jet boat and canoe, a rubber raft flexes with the tumbling stream. This ride was wild and surging, like clinging to a river bronc, as the bow dropped into troughs and the stern bucked sharply upward. People whooped and screamed when cold water rushed over the sides; Barry gunned the motor to stay in the main current, clear of rock outcrops and catching the big, deep waves. "Some pretty good hydraulics today," he said, as a burst of whirlpools went by, "but in the April runoff I've seen huge boils on the Thompson, and standing waves 15 feet high."

The canyon itself can be just as menacing, for often murderous landslides have roared down the cliffs. The worst came at Arthur Seat, where in 1905 a giant silt bench collapsed and briefly dammed the river. (Continued on page 184)

Lights gleam on mile-long Lion's Gate Bridge, the Trans-Canada's link with busy Vancouver. The bridge spans Burrard Inlet, a gateway for cruise ships to the Pacific as well as to the Inside Passage to Alaska. The Royal Princess (above) passes the wooded shores of thousand-acre Stanley Park fronting downtown Vancouver. With mountains and sea meeting in Vancouver, residents can ski in the morning, then sail in the afternoon in waters tempered by warm ocean currents.

Flower baskets brighten the wharf of Sea Village, a community of floating homes on Vancouver's Granville Island. At a summer barbecue, author and former CBC anchorman Stanley Burke (above, at left) toasts Roger Dahlquist, a resident of the seaside development Burke helped establish.

FOLLOWING PAGES: Giant watch ticks above the Swiss Pavilion at EXPO '86, where transportation and communication themes prevailed. Monorails whisked 22 million visitors through EXPO, which launched a tourism boom for Vancouver.

Staggering from his "tub" after two muscle-cramping hours, Jim Nunes begins a 100-yard wobble to the finish of Nanaimo's World Championship Bathtub Race. Each July a hundred or so boaters take on the 34-mile crossing of the Strait of Georgia from Nanaimo to Vancouver. Top prize: a gold bathtub plug.

In five minutes the water rose ten feet, flooding an upstream Indian village and taking 18 lives. We drifted by the slide tongue, a mass of rubble 80 feet high. "It might seem foolish to live in the canyon," Barry said, "but the fishing was good, and all the traders traveled here." He pointed to a faint track in the hills, the Cariboo Wagon Road. "It ran 400 miles north to the Cariboo goldfields. If this were the 1860s, you'd see covered wagons and camels there." The camels were a short-lived experiment: "They stank, and bit everything in sight. Couldn't walk far on the rocks, either."

Today the canyon carries two railway tracks and the Trans-Canada Highway, which in this stretch cost more than a million dollars a mile to build. As in Rogers Pass, the problem was avalanches—not of snow, but gravel. Rains here rush down rocky pinnacles and gravel banks, sweeping tons of debris toward the river. Rail tracks are protected by tunnels, rock-sheds, and several long stretches of chain mesh. In some places, highway engineers built retaining walls in the river channel, filled them with gravel, and laid a new roadbed on top.

But the road gives a wide berth to the acclaimed Jaws of Death. Barry had prepped us for this climax of our float with stories of giant whirlpools and shredded logs, of spring water levels far exceeding today's run of 25,000 cubic feet per second. "Just above the Jaws is an enormous whirlpool, and there's 15 good waves at the entrance. Right now it'll be fun, but in spring

you'd see a hole that would stand this boat on end." He cranked the motor and shot us safely forward into the buffeting descent of Jaws. The raft lunged from wave to wave, then suddenly we were through and pulling into slack water.

Below Lytton the van passed a confluence of waters as the clear Thompson met the turbid Fraser River. Longest stream in British Columbia, the Fraser rises far north on the Great Divide and flows a looping 850 miles to reach the Pacific at Vancouver. Still a wild, undammed river, the Fraser drains the upper plateau and provides its main transportation corridor. Along Fraser Canyon, the CP and CN Railways cling to opposite cliff walls—and at Ciska they switch sides, on crisscrossing trestles. The highway performs its own gymnastic feats, leaping creek ravines on single-span bridges and plunging through tunnels, eight in just one 20-mile stretch of canyon.

We were following the track of Simon Fraser, a fur trade surveyor who first descended this river in 1808 with voyageur canoes. After a three-year expedition across the Rockies, his journey nearly ended at the angry waters of Hells Gate. There the river channel contracts sharply, surmounted on both sides by sheer rock cliffs. The water discharge may reach 400,000 cubic feet per second, swirling into a giant vortex. ". . . it being absolutely impossible to carry the canoes by land," Fraser wrote, "all hands without hesitation embarked upon the mercy of this awful tide." They survived, but soon had to take to the cliffs, climbing rope ladders and narrow ledges "where no human being should venture."

On those heights today tourists will find a cable car that descends to the Hells Gate fudge shop, but I preferred to look down at the roiling water. Barry Burko said the current here was like "a plug pulled from a bathtub," yet against its force I saw the dark bodies of steelhead and salmon lunging upstream, driven by instinct to their spawning beds. Commercial fishing has greatly diminished the annual run, but the Fraser still remains the world's greatest salmon-producing river. To protect this resource, Hells Gate now embraces two massive concrete fishways. Inside, the fish swim in slower water and exit to quiet eddies, where they rest before going on. They must still pass native fishing banks, where in the span of a few days local tribes may net an entire winter's food.

We drove south at dusk, following the Fraser River through a valley between the Cascade and Coast ranges. The Trans-Canada was passing down the lower Cariboo Trail, a road to gold now bathed in amber light. The towns going by—Boston Bar, Dog Creek, Yale—began as wagon stations, places to rest horses and spend the night. Well-heeled miners stayed in hotels; others slept on "the soft side of the road," as one wrote in 1861. Built a century later, the national highway often had to fit a narrow shelf cut between railway and river. The road ran far ahead, a bright ribbon that reflected fading light. Cars sped by, flaunting bumper stickers: "Pass with Care—Driver Chewing Tobacco." "You are in Sasquatch Country." No doubt about it: the next travel trailer was labeled "Bigfoot."

At our campground in Hope I took a walk next morning and met Wilfred Brass, proud member of the Cree nation. "Good morning," he said. "Will you have some coffee?" He was emerging from a small tent; his family was still asleep in their motor home. "I can't sleep in that thing. Rather have my tent and the ground." With the coffee we ate bannock, flat bread that he dipped in sugar, and talked about our travels.

A native of northern Saskatchewan, Wilfred had seen a good part of the world. "The army stationed me in Korea, then later all over Canada. Now we go camping every summer, so I've seen a lot of the States." Down there he found mostly goodwill, but also some confusion about native people. "In California a man saw us eating bannock and asked if his son could come by to practice Spanish!"

At home, Wilfred holds a government post, working on social and economic development for his tribal band. "We are treaty Indians," he said, referring to their registration under the federal Indian Act, which covers more than 330,000 citizens. In the 1870s, Canadian Indians signed treaties that relinquished their traditional homelands in return for permanent reserves and other benefits. More than 70 percent still live on reserves or on public land, but migration to city jobs is growing.

"I have a daughter working for a degree in education and a cousin with a Ph.D. in psychology. We can't go back to the old subsistence ways." For the reserve Indians, people like Wilfred Brass work to protect land claims and veterans' rights, securing grants or loans that will improve tribal life. In his mind, one could follow modern ways without losing traditions. "The important thing is to define our culture," he said, "and culture means art, religion, or just taking time to socialize." So we poured another cup, talked awhile more, and wished each other well down the road.

From Hope to Vancouver is a fast 95 miles on the Trans-Canada, following the lower Fraser Valley below the Coast Mountains. Eons of gravel and mud washing down the river have formed a broad delta, now protected from floods by 120 miles of dikes. The rich soil and mild weather here promote intensive farming. Save for the mountain backdrop, we could have been in Wisconsin, passing fields of corn, hops, and grazing cattle. Much of this produce supplies greater Vancouver, home to some 1.3 million residents—or almost half of British Columbia. Just a century ago Vancouver was a frontier

saloon town, but today it has grown into Canada's third-largest city.

People flocked to Vancouver as it became a great commercial center, the western railway terminus and ocean harbor that opens Canada to Asia, but equally important was the city's grand natural setting. Around a peninsula of thrusting skyscrapers the sea has wrapped wide bays of blue water, and just beyond rise the white-crowned peaks of long coastal mountains. The Japanese Current tempers the climate: mild and rainy in winter; warm sunshine for the long summer days. Many have called Vancouver the most livable city in North America, famed for its clean streets and bustling marketplaces. And its reverence for outdoor beauty: At the city's waterfront lies Stanley Park, a thousand acres of tall red cedars, where beaches and cricket grounds adjoin displays of carved totem poles.

Vancouver has more museums, public gardens, and other attractions than we could easily see in a week. One afternoon we spent in silent awe with the mammoth carvings and painted masks of Northwest Coast Indians, a collection housed on the seaside campus of the University of British Columbia. But the big show in town was EXPO '86, a five-month exposition marking Vancouver's centennial and the world's progress in transportation and communication. After months of continuous travel across a big, uncrowded country, I was a bit numbed by this urban extravaganza, which packed scores of pavilions, theaters, restaurants, and shops into 175 acres along the shore of False Creek, a protected ocean inlet.

Some 22 million visitors came to EXPO during its 165-day run, patiently lining up for hours to tour displays that often featured giant movie screens and glittery special effects. Images would dip, soar, and glide across a bank of video monitors, controlled by computer wizardry. Equally long lines waited for meals or snacks, entertained by street musicians carrying steel drums

and guitars. One avant-garde group explored the acoustics of bicycle spokes, hammered with knives and chopsticks. At each pavilion, crowds gathered with souvenir "passports" to obtain a colorful inked stamp. Often this image inversely related to its country's size: tiny Brunei filled one entire page.

In a few days we quickly spun through much of Europe and Asia, a smorgasbord of sight and sound that seemed well-suited to a place known as False Creek. From high-speed trains and futuristic autos we slipped into Cuba, where the U.S. visitors were buying up long-embargoed cigars. Australians bade us endless "G'days" and bragged about their America's Cup—which they lost, several months later. Everyone was gazing brightly at the future, promising faster deliveries and bigger payloads, but the United Nations took another view of progress. Its somber displays reported that nations have fought 150 wars since 1945; that today they spend an average $20,000 to train each soldier, but only $380 to educate a child.

For me, some brighter views appeared at Canadian pavilions, which recalled the land and the faces I had met on my cross-country journey. Prince Edward Island and Nova Scotia, an appropriately small exhibit, displayed sand dunes and ferryboats. Quebec took me back to maple leaves and the streets of Montreal; Ontario showed fleets of long canoes, crossing many waters. Then Saskatchewan, wide fields of wheat and barley; Alberta, a land of dinosaurs and chuck wagon races; and the host, British Columbia, glacial streams with leaping salmon. I saw a new destination in some pictures of the Northwest Territories, with captions by native spokesmen: "We have no word in our language for wilderness, as everywhere we go is home."

To Vancouver, EXPO was a giant festival,

most of it torn down after closing in late 1986. A more lasting project has arisen just across False Creek at Granville Island, a once shabby industrial site now redeveloped into a flourishing waterside community. Most visitors come to shop in Granville's public markets for fresh-baked breads and smoked salmon, but the island—a peninsula, really—also has playgrounds and cafés, galleries, live theaters, offices, and an art college. Also a hotel, but I was calling at Sea Village, a cluster of floating homes ranked along a wharf.

My host was Stanley Burke, who cheerfully showed me about his airy, comfortable digs—paneled walls and skylit ceilings, along with certain waterborne necessities: "Would you like to see the bilge pumps?" Later we sat on his deck, partaking of cold Canadian ale as the house gently swayed in the wake of passing boats. It must be pleasant to sit here with a drink at rush hour, when the city is emptying out and cars crawl across the bridge for houses far out in the 'burbs. Stanley took a long, meditative pull on his Molson. "Well . . . ," he said slowly, "frankly, it is."

The tone was not complacent, just satisfied with today's better times, rather like Granville Island. For a dozen years Stanley was a foreign correspondent and chief anchor on Canada's national television news, a face that reported the daily ration of wars and riots to millions of living rooms. A difference over news policies led to his resignation. He wrote, traveled, then came back to his hometown of Vancouver. With some friends he helped form Sea Village. Today he owns a newspaper on Vancouver Island, a place he dearly loves. "But I live here because of this house and the neighbors, a marvelous old collection of water rats."

The end of August had come, another school year beginning, so Bonnie and Jeff flew home from Vancouver while I continued west. In a few more days my trip would end as well, but not before I had followed the Trans-Canada to Vancouver Island. On a car ferry that crossed

Yachts tie up in front of the ivy-covered Empress Hotel, a Victoria showpiece since 1908. Afternoon teas evoke a bit of England for hotel guests, often lured to Victoria for its idyllic sailing and world-class fishing. The Strait of Georgia rewards fishermen off Stuart Island with a 30-pound salmon (above). At day's end, the charter boat Pleasure Dome (below) prepares to set sail.

the Strait of Georgia, I joined a small crew of hardy souls on the open deck. Propped against the bulkhead, we endured an hour of buffeting winds to watch the sun set. Fishing boats passed, hauling seines through the salmon-rich waters. More than 20 million salmon are caught here annually, most in the busy weeks of fall. Five thousand miles east of here, I reckoned, salmon were also rising up fast Atlantic streams.

I was in a sense coming full circle, having gone from sea to sea and ending my trip as it had begun, on a big offshore island. Ringed by tidal waters, islands have their own ways and means, which no visitor can long alter. I spent my first night on Vancouver Island at Nanaimo, a busy port that each year stages a mid-July frolic, the World Championship Bathtub Race. Contestants make the 34-mile run from Nanaimo to Vancouver in homemade boats, tub-shaped with outboard motors. Some entrants don clown wigs and fill the tubs with soapy lather, then gamely vie for the top prize, a gold bathtub plug. This evening a pair of needle-nosed sea kayaks went slipping across the harbor, past ranks of moored yachts and launches.

At Nanaimo I detoured from the Trans-Canada for a 110-mile drive across the island to its western shore. The road led from harbor villages up into a mountainous interior, covered with lush rain forest. At once a misty shower descended, for these heights catch the first moist winds coming off the Pacific. The trees were Douglas firs, regal forms with no lower branches, their straight trunks reaching 200 feet and more. Cathedral Grove, a roadside park, offered a path through specimen trees, some more than 800 years old. Just two centuries after the Vikings reached Newfoundland, these trees first lifted toward the sun. They altered its light to a dim silver-gray, bathed the air with a strong evergreen scent. Nothing seemed to die here; from fallen logs, seedlings had already risen.

Coming down from the Mackenzie Range, I saw at last the broad flat sweep of ocean. At Pacific Rim National Park, long combers were rolling in across a white sand beach. The day was cool; only a few walkers strolled in the surf with cuffs rolled. Business was slow for the lifeguard; he had sunk into his earphones, eyes hidden by a pair of shades. I stared awhile at the far horizon, a landless arc of gray. I had run out of Canada here, reached its final shore. From a pack I took a bottle, scooped up some Pacific, and doused the van's front tires. Thus ended the rite that launched my trip, back on Atlantic shores.

That night my camping neighbors were Everet and Eleanor Near, a couple on the road after years of farming in western Saskatchewan. "My Dad homesteaded our place in 1910," Everet said, "and now we've passed it to our son and grandsons. That's a fourth generation on the land." The Nears planned to use their motor home to see a wide slice of North America. "We spend four months each winter in Arizona—play golf and cards, go dancing or eat out," said Eleanor. "Down there they call us snowbirds." Many fellow Canadians join them, migrating with the seasons like flocks of geese. Going easily back and forth across our borders, the Nears have become great admirers of the States, strong proponents of freer trade: "Do you ever see a day," they asked, "when we might become one country?" One continent, I thought, but always two distinct countries.

A day later I took the Trans-Canada down the island's east coast to Victoria, the genteel capital of British Columbia. No town west of London could seem more British, with its traditions of high tea and lawn bowling, double-decker buses and cozy pubs. Yet Britain never knew this temperate Pacific climate, the months of cool rain and warm sunshine in which rose gardeners revel. For Victoria blooms nearly year-round, abounding in public parks with banks of flowers and thick, glossy lawns, and in thousands of hanging baskets that bedeck the city's streets and shops with splashes of color.

Gardening is Victoria's communal passion. A popular radio show devotes hours to callers' questions on soil mix and insect pests, while nearly every home displays its window boxes and heaping beds of roses, lilies, or rainbow-hued petunias. For horticultural inspiration, visitors may trek 14 miles north to Butchart Gardens, the product of one woman's determined efforts to build a floral extravaganza. In 1905, Jenny Butchart began to surround her estate home with formal gardens—some 50 acres. Her greatest challenge was to convert an old limestone quarry into a sunken garden. To cover the barren rock walls, she rappelled down in a bosun's chair and calmly planted ivy.

Today, visitors to Butchart Gardens may wander past star-shaped pools and pluming fountains, as the annual pageant of seasons unfolds. Spring tulips and azaleas give way to summer daisies and dense, showy begonias; the dusky autumn foliage passes into a brief winter, when evergreens stand sentinel. The grounds include places to rest and dine, enjoy a cabaret show and an evening fireworks display. In her day, Jenny Butchart provided tea for all visitors, and often invited groups to supper. A good deal of that hospitality still prevails. To visitors on night walks, a leaflet gently advises: "If all the lights are shining directly in your eyes, look behind you. You may discover that you are walking around the gardens in the wrong direction."

I had my own troubles navigating in Victoria, where the streets kept running into ocean. Seated at the end of Saanich Peninsula, Victoria looks south across the Strait of Juan de Fuca to Washington State, a brief ferry ride away. Yet this provincial capital has carved out its own peculiar time and space, somewhere between a nostalgia for Ye Olde England and an affinity for

the wide Pacific realm. Here I might step into the Tudor past, at a reproduction of Anne Hathaway's cottage, or stroll past shops offering bone china and wool tartans to the Crystal Gardens, just in time for high tea. Armed with a pile of scones and toasted crumpets, I could linger beside a glassed-in tropical Pacific garden, a collection of exotic palms and ferns where parrots roost amid banana trees and wild ginger plants.

Victoria is North America's last outpost of European settlement, one of its first ports of call for Asian travelers. Many of the town's visitors were Japanese, cameras ever trained on the gardens and public buildings, especially when lit at night. At the water's edge rests Parliament, its Victorian dome and cupolas outlined with arcade-like strings of light bulbs. On my last evening in western Canada, I drove past this landmark in search of Beacon Hill Park, official end of the Trans-Canada Highway. Finally I found a marker: "Mile 0," it read, though for me it represented many thousand more.

Ahead of me, Amer and Michelle Manzur sat in a camper van bearing New York plates. We said hello, discovered that at home we lived but 50 minutes apart. Their lives had begun in Pakistan and Russia, respectively, so we had all traveled far to reach this intersection. Both mechanical engineers, they often changed jobs to get time for the road. "We did 24,000 miles in Europe one year," Amer explained, "and so far this trip in Canada and the States has been 17,000." Michelle ticked off the states and provinces they had toured, tripling my own puny ventures. "Maybe we have a little gypsy blood," she laughed. How had they liked Canada? "Oh, so much beauty, so big and open and free. We want to go far north now, till we can see the white nights."

So did I, one day. At Mile 0 we shook hands and said bon voyage. I had journeyed across a wide country, from Signal Hill to Beacon Hill; now it was time to turn for home.

ADDITIONAL READING

Readers may consult the *National Geographic Index* for related books and articles and refer to the following publications:

GENERAL: F. J. Anderson, *Natural Resources in Canada*; Margaret Bemister, *Thirty Indian Legends of Canada*; J. Brian Bird, *The Natural Landscapes of Canada*; Stephen S. Birdsall and John W. Florin, *Regional Landscapes of the United States and Canada*; June Callwood, *Portrait of Canada*; Ella E. Clark, *Indian Legends of Canada*; S. D. Clark, *The Developing Canadian Community*; Ramsay Cook, *Canada: A Modern Study*; Donald G. Creighton, *A History of Canada*; Peter Dobell, *Canada's Search for New Roles*; James Doyle, *Yankees in Canada: A Collection of Nineteenth-Century Travel Narratives*; Jean Leonard Elliott (ed.), *Two Nations, Many Cultures: Ethnic Groups in Canada*; R. Douglas Francis and Donald B. Smith, *Readings in Canadian History*; Northrop Frye, *Divisions on a Ground: Essays on Canadian Culture*; Joel Garreau, *The Nine Nations of North America*; John W. Holmes, *Life with Uncle: The Canadian-American Relationship*; Hurtig Publishers, *The Canadian Encyclopedia*; Robert S. Kane, *Canada A to Z*; Edward McCourt, *The Road Across Canada*; Andrew H. Malcolm, *The Canadians*; Geoffrey Matthews and Robert Morrow, *Canada and the World: An Atlas Resource*; Brian Milne, *Trans-Canada Country*; J. H. Paterson, *North America: A Geography of Canada and the United States*; R. Pomfred, *The Economic Development of Canada*; Marylee Stephenson, *Canada's National Parks: A Visitor's Guide*; John Warkentin (ed.), *Canada: A Geographical Interpretation*; Edmund Wilson, *O Canada: An American's Notes on Canadian Culture*.

ATLANTIC PROVINCES: Michael Collie, *New Brunswick*; Jean Daigle (ed.), *The Acadians of the Maritimes: Thematic Studies*; Millie Evans and Eric Mullen, *Our Maritimes*; R. C. Harris and John Warkentin, *Canada Before Confederation*; Pat and Jim Lotz, *Cape Breton Island*; W. S. MacNutt, *The Atlantic Provinces: The Emergence of Colonial Society*; Frederick Pratson, *Guide to Eastern Canada*; Frank Underhill, *The Image of Confederation*; P. B. Waite, *The Life and Times of Confederation, 1864-1867*.

QUEBEC: Ramsay Cook, *The Maple Leaf Forever*; Donald G. Creighton, *The Empire of the St. Lawrence*; Benoi Deschênes, *The Magic Gouge: Wood Sculpture*; R. C. Harris, *The Seigneurial System in Early Canada: A Geographical Study*; Cornelius Jaenen, *The Role of the Church in New France*; Hugh MacLennan, *Two Solitudes*; Francis Parkman, *The Old Regime in Canada*; Henry D. Thoreau, *A Yankee in Canada*; Susan M. Trofimenkoff, *The Dream of Nation: A Social and Intellectual History of Quebec*; Mason Wade, *The French Canadians, 1760-1967*.

ONTARIO: Harold Innis, *The Fur Trade in Canada: An Introduction to Canadian Economic History*; J. K. Johnson, *Historical Essays on Upper Canada*; Bill Mason, *Path of the Paddle*; Barbara Moon, *The Canadian Shield*; Joan Murray, *The Best of Tom Thomson*.

PRAIRIE PROVINCES: Menno Boldt and J. A. Long, *The Quest for Justice: Aboriginal Peoples and Aboriginal Rights*; J. F. Conway, *The West: The History of a Region in Confederation*; Gerald Friesen, *The Canadian Prairies: A History*; Freda Hawkins, *Canada and Immigration*; S. W. Horrall, *The Pictorial History of the Royal Canadian Mounted Police*; Howard Palmer, *The Settlement of the West*; G.F.G. Stanley, *Louis Riel*; James T. Teller (ed.), *Natural History of Manitoba: Legacy of the Ice Age*.

THE CORDILLERA: D. M. Baird, *Banff National Park*; Esther Fraser, *The Canadian Rockies*; Brian Patton, *Parkways of the Canadian Rockies*; Robert Scharff, *Canada's Mountain National Parks*.

THE PACIFIC REALM: G.P.V. and Helen B. Akrigg, *British Columbia Chronicle 1778-1846: Adventures By Sea and Land*; Marjorie M. Halpin, *Totem Poles: An Illustrated Guide*; S. W. Jackson, *Vancouver Island*; Della Kew and P. E. Goddard, *Indian Art and Culture of the Northwest Coast*; Eric Nicol, *Vancouver*; Hilary Stewart, *Looking at Indian Art of the Northwest Coast*; Morris Zaslow, *The Opening of the Canadian North*.

JOHN G. AGNONE, N.G.S. STAFF, AND MARGARET G. HUBBARD

GOVERNOR GENERAL'S FOOT GUARD EVOKES CANADA'S BRITISH TIES.

ACKNOWLEDGMENTS

The Special Publications Division is grateful for the assistance of our project consultants: Alec C. McEwen, International Boundary Commission; Burk Frebold, Transport Canada; and Shig Uyeyama, Canadian Embassy. Agencies frequently consulted included the provincial tourism offices; Department of Indian Affairs and Northern Development; Energy, Mines, and Resources Canada; Parks Canada; St. Lawrence Seaway Development Corporation; Statistics Canada.

We also wish to acknowledge the assistance of many other organizations and individuals named or quoted in the text and those cited here: Sid Andrews, Loraine D. Bailey, Stephen Bartlett, Roger Beardmore, Jill Biggins, Norm O. Blackburn, Keith Bocking, Marc Chabot, Marilyn Chandler, Ian Church, Ted Cisaroski, Iva Clark, François Côté, Celes Davar, Natalie Davis, Perry Davis, Paul DeMone, Margaret Doody, Sharon Doucette, Allan M. Doyle, Jonathan Fenton, Evelyn Friesen, Michel Gagnon, Steve Gallant, Karen Garland, Inès Gonzales, Michel Harvey, David Huddlestone, Mart Johanson, Mike Joy, Paul Kennedy, Faye Kerr, Joe Kowalski, Marie LaCabanne, Anne Lacasse, Sharon Larter, Michael Leahy, Jean-Marc Lessard, Leo LeVasseur, Ken Lozinsky, Andrea Lukie, Dave MacEachern, Donald MacInnis, Milissa McLean, John McPhee, Alan McTavish, Gerard Makuch, Debbie Marsh, Margaret May, Joyce Meyer, John Miller, Charles Moss, Neil Muhtadi, Angie Neary, Helen Jean Newman, Cheryl Nielsen, Chris Page, Nicole Paiement, Kaye Parker, Leila Philip, Bill Phillips, Mike Pinay, Bob Plaster, Liz Plett, Marcia Porter, Elvira Quarin, Sonya Ralph-Bandy, Lianne Roberts, Elizabeth Saunders, Roxane Scheler, Elaine Showalter, J.W. Stephens, Roy Stephens, Peggy Stewart, Dan Strickland, Stephen Suddes, Dan Sullivan, Guy Tanguay, Linda Thornton, Jim Todgham, Ray Troke, Greg Udod, Mary Ader Upstone, John Walper, Keith Webb, Keith White, Mike Whittle, Roger Wilson, Ron Winbow, and David Youngston.

Index

Boldface indicates illustrations; *italic* refers to picture captions.

Library of Congress CIP Data
Howarth, William L., 1940-
Traveling the Trans-Canada.

Bibliography: p.
Includes index.
1. Canada—Description and travel—1981- 2. Howarth, William L., 1940- —Journeys—Canada. I. Title.

F1017.H68 1987	917.1'046	87-28145
ISBN 0-87044-626-6 (regular edition)		ISBN 0-87044-631-2 (library edition)

Composition for *Traveling the Trans-Canada: From Newfoundland to British Columbia* by the Typographic section of National Geographic Production Services, Pre-Press Division. Printed and bound by Holladay-Tyler Printing Corp., Rockville, Md. Film preparation by Catharine Cooke Studio, Inc., New York, N.Y. Color separations by Lanman Progressive Company, Washington, D.C.; Lincoln Graphics, Inc., Cherry Hill, N.J.; and NEC, Inc., Nashville, Tenn.